DANCE FOR ME WHEN I DIE

A book in the series LATIN AMERICA IN TRANSLATION /
EN TRADUCCIÓN / EM TRADUÇÃO

Sponsored by the Duke–University of North Carolina
Program in Latin American Studies

DANCE FOR ME WHEN I DIE

Cristian Alarcón · *Translated by Nick Caistor and Marcela López Levy*

Duke University Press
Durham and London 2019

© 2019 Duke University Press
All rights reserved
Printed in the United States of America on acid-free paper ∞
Designed by Courtney Leigh Baker
Typeset in Garamond Premier Pro by Copperline Book Services

Cataloging-in-Publication Data is available from the Library
of Congress

ISBN 9781478003144 (hardcover : alk. paper)
ISBN 9781478003786 (pbk. : alk. paper)
ISBN 9781478004417 (ebook)

COVER ART: Alfredo Srur, photograph from the series *Geovany
no quiere ser Rambo*, 2001. Courtesy of the artist.

To the Alarcón family · To the Casanova family

The traitor lives between two loyalties; he lives a double life, in disguise. He must pretend, remain in the wasteland of treachery, sustained by the impossible dreams of a future where his vile acts will at last be rewarded. But in what way will the vile acts of the traitor be rewarded in the future? —RICARDO PIGLIA, *Respiración artificial*

I call violence an audacity at rest but in love with dangers. It can be seen in a look, a way of walking, a smile, and you are the ones in whom it makes waves. It disconcerts you. This violence is a calm that disturbs you. —JEAN GENET, *The Thief's Journal*

What characterizes the concept of adventure and sets it apart from all the fragments of life . . . is the fact that something isolated and accidental may correspond to a need and contain a meaning. —GEORG SIMMEL, "The Adventure"

CONTENTS

FOREWORD · *Javier Auyero and Gabriela Polit-Dueñas*

Dance for Me When I Die was originally published in 2004 in Spanish—first in Argentina, and then in Chile and Colombia. Now in its thirtieth printing, it has become a mandatory text in high schools and colleges across Argentina and the object of numerous reviews and discussions. In vivid, luminous prose this book engages with topics that are at the forefront of political and cultural debates in contemporary Latin America: urban violence, marginality, youth, and precarity, to name just a few. Readers of the English version of this book will discover a slice of life in urban Latin America that has been the object of much misunderstanding—and not a few simplified representations. They will also, we believe, feel compelled to consider the merit of the *crónica* and the form's potential to narrate social life in its polychromatic dimensions.

During the first decades of the twenty-first century, most Latin American countries have witnessed an increase in urban violence; Latin America is the only region in the world that, without being at war, is experiencing an increase in lethal violence, as measured in homicide rates. This violence, analysts agree, is not evenly distributed across social and geographic space but is concentrated in territories where the urban poor dwell—known as *favelas, barrios, comunas,* or *villas* in different countries of the subcontinent.[1] Journalists and scholars also agree that within these poor urban areas, different forms of violence (between family members, intimate partners, or community residents) converge and define the texture of everyday life. Social-scientific studies point to a number of factors associated with the ubiquitous violence in low-income neighborhoods: inequality, youth unemployment, the illicit drug trade, and the fragile legitimacy of the state's monopoly on violence. Many of these studies, however, still lack a thorough understanding of the uses and forms of such violence, of its lived experience, and of the ways in which both victims and perpetrators make sense of it.

Depictions of poor people's lives offered by the social sciences frequently condense entire, and quite diverse, categories (the urban poor, young poor men, poor women) to one or two salient portrayals (single mother, welfare recipient, sex worker, drug dealer, gang member). Sometimes with the author's best intentions or because of the imperative of making a more or less sophisticated social-scientific argument, these portrayals shrink complex and fluctuating lives to narrow explanations. Patricia Fernandez-Kelly summarized this tendency in straightforward terms for the case of studies of poverty in the United States: "Impoverished people in general and African Americans in particular have been reduced to flattened representations of social problems" (2015, 10).

In the Latin American literary tradition, crónicas—of the kind provided in this book—have attempted to overcome these simplifications by restoring complexity to the urban popular world (and to a great extent they have succeeded). Since its inception as a modern genre, the crónica has been a critical and unofficial political narrative that gives broader accounts of the region's tensions. Readers have encountered a combination of political criticism and aesthetically elaborated prose in the early depictions of modern cities, from the crónicas of José Martí, Julián del Casal, and Manuel Gutiér-

---

1 The stratification of urban violence is hardly a Latin American phenomenon. "Rivalries between Chicago's increasingly splintered gangs and cliques over sales of heroin, Ecstasy, prescription drugs and marijuana have given way to gunfire," writes *New York Times* reporter Monica Davey (2016). Citywide, homicides increased 56 percent between 2015 and 2016, but "just five of Chicago's 22 police districts are driving the bulk of Chicago's rise." These are all in the poorest South and West Sides. The 11th district, located on the city's West Side, witnessed an 89 percent increase in homicides—ninety-one people were killed between January 1 and December 6, 2016.

rez Nájera, to Roberto Arlt's "Aguafuertes porteñas" and Salvador Novo's images of Mexico City, to the journalistic works of Gabriel García Márquez; from Rodolfo Walsh's denunciation of state brutality in the 1950s in Argentina to Elena Poniatowska's collective account of the student movement and massacre of Tlatelolco in 1968; from Alonso Salazar's appalling stories of Medellín's comuna dwellers to the crude realities of underground life in Pedro Lemebel's Santiago de Chile. And, of course, there is the great Carlos Monsiváis, who wrote about Mexico's underworld with the same passion with which he wrote about his country's countless political conflicts using a prose that masterfully expresses sophisticated ideas in a colloquial language. These crónicas combine ethnographic work, literary style, political denunciation, social analysis, and, in many cases, a close-up description of the forms and effects of violence.[2]

Readers familiar with Salazar's and Lemebel's work will find resemblances in *Dance for Me When I Die*. Like Salazar, Cristian Alarcón explores the predicament of young men who have normalized the fact that they will die early in life. These young men are being killed not only by state actors but also by other young men just like them. As with epic heroes, the familiarity with death, these *cronistas* tell us, does not prevent the young urban dwellers from being afraid of their tragic fate. To show the complexity of this quandary, Alarcón—like Lemebel—narrates the story in the language of these young men. Herein lies the uniqueness of the book into which you are about to delve: understanding the vernacular language of the *villa*—its rhythms and pauses, its graciousness and grotesque allusions, its humor and pain—places readers closer to the complex and heterogeneous lives of poor people in one of the most violent areas of Greater Buenos Aires. The work that Alarcón does with the local language shows that knowledge can build empathy.

Following in the literary tradition of García Márquez's *Chronicle of a Death Foretold*, *Dance for Me When I Die* begins and ends with the death of Frente Vital—a local Robin Hood figure whose ethics and affective connections to the shantytown determine his life as a thief. Frente is already dead

---

2 While the aestheticization of the real and the hybridity of the genre might make readers think of crónicas as *testimonios*, there are important differences between the two. The inception and expansion of modern crónicas has to be understood in relationship with the development of journalism in the region. Crónicas were also instrumental in the autonomization of the literary field; see Mahieux 2011, Ramos 1989, and Rotker 1992.

by the time Alarcón arrives at the villa, and yet the cronista places him at the center of his search. Conducting challenging fieldwork in the villa over more than eighteen months, Alarcón gathered testimonies from Frente's friends and foes, his lovers, his mother, and his siblings. In reconstructing Frente's life and death, Alarcón gives a profound account of the local culture. At the same time, he writes himself into the story and offers readers his own tentative discoveries of how villa dwellers act, think, and feel in the most dire of circumstances.

A storyteller rises up against the widespread indifference—and hostility—toward those living at the bottom of the Latin American sociosymbolic order and illuminates the lives, sufferings, and hopes of the wretched of the city. In so doing, Alarcón joins a long and respected tradition in the region's literary history.

References

Davey, Monica. 2016. "In Chicago, Bodies Pile Up at Intersection of 'Depression and Rage.'" *New York Times*, December 9. https://www.nytimes.com/2016/12/09/us/chicago-shootings-district-11.html?_r=0.

Fernandez-Kelly, Patricia. 2015. *The Hero's Fight: African Americans in West Baltimore and the Shadow of the State*. Princeton, NJ: Princeton University Press.

Mahieux, Vivianne. 2011. *Urban Chronicles in Modern Latin America: The Shared Intimacy of Everyday Life*. Austin: University of Texas Press.

Ramos, Julio. 1989. *Desencuentros de la modernidad en América Latina: Literatura y política en el siglo XIX*. Mexico City: Fondo de Cultura Económica.

Rotker, Susana. 1992. *La invención de la crónica*. Buenos Aires: Ediciones Letra Buena.

ACKNOWLEDGMENTS

It would have been impossible for me to finish this book without the conversations I had with my friends, without their infinite generosity in allowing me, many a time, to go on and on about everything I couldn't quite see and understand. I am grateful for the patience of Lucas Mac Guire and Pepe Matrás; of Antonia Portaneri and Jorge Jaunarena; of Gabriel Giubellino, Marta Dillon, Josefina Giglio, Raquel Robles, María Zago, Romina Tomillo, Marcelo Chávez, Graciela Mochkofsky, Gabriel Pasquini, Ricardo Ragendorfer. To Flavio Rapidardi. To my colleagues at *Página/12*, where I began to write this story. To my colleagues at Asociación Miguel Bru, for forgiving so many absences while I was working on it. To María del Carmen Verdú, who once told me that young thieves had a saint. To the lawyer Andrea Sajnovsky and everyone who dared to speak out during the investigation into the Death Squad. Also Maximiliano Barañao for his sweet company. For the hospitality of his family during the time I spent in Concepción de Uruguay. To the refuge offered by the Carey family in Brazil. Thank you for having been with me in the slum, Alfredo Santiago Srur; and thank you for getting me out that night in the wee hours. I am also grateful to Marina Enríquez, María Moreno, Silvia Delfino, and Claudio Zeiger. Each of their readings also helped create this account.

When I first arrived in the shantytown, all I knew was that here, in the northern outskirts of Buenos Aires, some fifteen blocks from San Fernando station, a crime had taken place and a new pagan idol had been born in its wake. The Bonaerense, the local police force, had gunned down seventeen-year-old gang member Víctor Manuel Vital—known as "Frente," or "Forehead." Hiding beneath a table in one of the neighborhood shacks, he had been shouting to them not to shoot—that he was handing himself in. After his death, he had become a special kind of saint to the generation who survived him: they considered him so powerful that he could make bullets swerve and save gang members from shrapnel.

Between the ages of thirteen and seventeen, Frente became famous for his youth, for his generosity with the loot he acquired by pointing his .32-caliber revolver, for resurrecting the old code of honor among thieves that had long been buried by a habit of betrayal, and for always being on the front lines. The life and death of Víctor Vital, and the daily lives of the survivors from the shantytowns of that outer ring of the city—the hoods of San Francisco, of 25 de Mayo, and of La Esperanza—are inroads into those communities that at first appear hostile, responding warily, like an abused animal, to the sight of an approaching stranger. Invoking Frente's name was the sole passport that allowed me access to the narrow alleyways and turfs, to the secrets and veiled truths, to the intensity that stirs and dances to the *cumbia* beat in an area that from a distance may look like a neighborhood but close up is just a tangle of dirty alleyways.[1]

Perhaps it would have been better for my journalism career if I'd pursued a different story—revealing the identity of a murderer, the mechanics of an execution, a message from the Mafia, the power network behind a corrupt cop, a crime of passion committed with a sharpened blade. Following each of these stories, I could have made a denunciation and tracked the judicial attempts to establish what attorneys call "criminal responsibility" and journalists, "material proof." But one day I found myself trying awkwardly to follow the swinging rhythm of the young thieves from San Fernando, sitting for hours on the same street corner, watching how they played soccer and kicked the hell out of a hopeless midfielder. I immersed myself in another kind of language and time, in other ways of surviving, living until it is time to face your own death. I grew to know the shantytown until I shared its pain.

As time went by and asphalt and urbanization encroached, the shantytown of San Francisco—and 25 de Mayo to the north and La Esperanza to the south—was converted into an official district. New streets were laid out and old shacks bulldozed to make way for cement and order, replacing the natural chaos of the unplanned neighborhood. But the grid plan manages to convey the fleeting impression of a neighborhood only through the efforts of homeowners who have worked hard to keep up appearances despite their poverty. It provides the slum with a pleasant veneer, but behind each of these well-kept house fronts run alleyways lined with precarious tin shacks reinforced with makeshift brick or cinder-block walls. Between the 25 de Mayo and La Esperanza neighborhoods, part of the old shantytown remains intact, with shacks crammed together around four internal alleyways. It was in one of these alleys—the one off General Pinto Street, only a block from his home—that Frente Vital was murdered on the morning of February 6, 1999.

Gradually, I was able to explore farther. I managed to penetrate the drug dens, the homes of older, retired criminals, the hideouts. At first, I could ex-

---

1 *Cumbia* is a popular dance originally from Colombia and Panama. In Argentina, it has been influenced by local genres such as *chamamé*, and the best known form is *cumbia villera*, cumbia from the shantytowns, which is easily identified by its lyrics about drugs, alcohol, sex, and delinquency.—Trans.

plore only the block where Frente lived. I observed how, at mealtimes, the women began to borrow methodically from their lifelong neighbors—half a cup of oil from one shack, a bit of rice from another, an onion, a precious piece of meat from farther down. Mothers searching for whatever they could find to stave off hunger crossed from street to street; needing urgently to satiate their family's grumbling stomachs, they recovered scraps to recycle with a skill acquired from years of working every day to fill the pot.

Frente was buried in a plot in the poorest part of the San Fernando cemetery, where the imposing mausoleums at the entrance stand alongside simple earthen burials. Adorned with plastic flowers, the dead seem to have been sown across a flat expanse now dominated by Víctor Vital's grave. Groups of kids wearing stylish sweats and the latest sneakers frequently gather there to share weed and beer with Frente. The offerings they leave in return for his protection mark out his grave from the rest.

San Fernando is the district on the outskirts of Buenos Aires with one of the last train stops before Tigre; it sits close to the banks of the Plate River, between Beccar and Carupá. It's the part of Argentina where the gulf between rich and poor is most extreme, where hunger and opulence rub shoulders. The riches of others are there for the taking.

Two years after my arrival in the hood, the youths who are coming of age without the distinct rules set in place by Frente Vital now steal from old women and young kids in the area. They're after ten pesos for their next fix of false grandeur. They're no longer content to assert their identity through the forbidden status offered by famous brands; instead, they seek the artificial paradise of a bag of glue or the intoxication of pills designed to calm the nerves of the middle class, pills washed down with the worst wine sold by the local storekeeper, who sooner or later they will attack as well, simply because times have changed, everything is against them, and there is no law. No one is equal; there is no miracle of salvation.

As if he and his mystical powers comprised both condemnation and salvation, the myth of Frente Vital for me opened the door to the ugly realization that his death portended in his community both his sanctification and the end of an era. The account that follows is an attempt to illustrate and recount that end, as well as the start of an age when there will be no one like Frente Vital to turn to for protection from police harassment, or from the traitors who, like hunger, cast a looming shadow over everyday life in the slums.

I

María had her hands in a tub of soapy water when she heard the worst news of her life.

"Guys, come on! Let's go! The cops are all over the place—it looks like they've got Frente!"

María was washing a pair of jeans in the yard of her boyfriend Chaías's place. She had been living there for a couple of weeks after an argument with her stepdad, a lowlife dealer who belonged to the Chanos clan.

"Guys! It looks like they've killed Frente!"

The kids from the block, which looked like a decent neighborhood from the outside but was really just a bunch of alleyways, all ran out at once. But María didn't move. She didn't look around or react in any way. She had had a short but intense relationship with Frente that was already over. She felt ashamed to feel the way she did or to react how she wanted to react. Instead, she told herself: "I'll just play dumb." She figured that if anything really bad had happened, somebody was bound to come tell her. And so she pretended to carry on washing the clothes, resisting the urge to run too, faster than anyone, desperate to see the fate that had befallen the boy she still loved.

"They've killed Frente," said a woman on the other side of the fence some ten minutes later.

María absorbed the news. She'd always known that it could happen someday, but she never thought it would be so soon: she was just thirteen, and Frente was seventeen. She remembered those lengthy love letters about a future that seemed like the only one imaginable, even though now she was with someone else, even though her new boyfriend was one of Víctor's friends, even though the world now seemed like it might collapse all around her. Drying her hands on her jeans, she left the yard and walked three blocks, crossed the empty field, and went into the 25 de Mayo slum, heading straight for her mother's shack—the same one she had escaped to take refuge at Chaías's place. As soon as she entered, she threw herself into her mother's arms as she hadn't for a long time.

"Mom, come with me—I think they've killed Frente," she sobbed into her mother's shoulder.

COVERED BY NOTHING but a thin sheet, Laura was nevertheless sweltering from the humidity that, even at ten-thirty in the morning, heralded a coming storm. She was exhausted after a night at Club Tropitango with Frente, the girls, and the rest of his friends who were still at large, when she was woken by a din unusual for a Saturday morning, a commotion that somehow signaled the coming battle. Without so much as a "good morning," her mother told her, in a firm but kind voice:

"Lau, I think they've killed Frente."

Laura got out of bed feeling numb, oblivious to the heaviness of her body after the late night, the bottles of alcohol they had drunk as they danced again and again in the middle of the dance floor to the tortuous ballads of Leo Mattioli and his band. She walked the short length of alleyway between her and the deserted field from which she could see into the narrow entrance to the slum. Someone shouted:

"The place is crawling with cops! You'd think they were after Gordo Valor!"[1]

Víctor's closest friends crept as near as they could to the shack where he

---

[1] Luis "El Gordo" Valor was a notorious bank robber in Buenos Aires during the 1990s. Caught and imprisoned in 1994, he succeeded in escaping from jail and became a popular hero. He was recaptured, then released, and finally imprisoned again in 2014. —Trans.

had been cornered. They had heard the shots. A few people had caught a glimpse of Víctor and, behind him, Luisito and Coqui, two of the members of Los Bananita, running through the heart of the 25 de Mayo slum with the police sirens wailing in the background, crossing the empty lot that borders the San Francisco slum, and disappearing down one of the alleys into Doña Inés's shack. Thanks to the slum's speedy rumor mill, they knew that Coqui was captured halfway down the street when he tried to hide in the entrance to an apartment block instead of continuing to run. Since the moment the shots had been fired, there had been no more hint of what had taken place. No one knew if Luis and Frente were still alive. As more police reinforcements piled in, they tried to convince the neighbors to stay back.

MAURO EDGED HIS way forward between the shacks and managed to climb onto the roof of the shack—now surrounded by a squad of cops—where Víctor, alias Frente, and his buddy Luisito had tried to take shelter. Mauro was one of Frente's closest friends, a leading member of the previous generation of gang members who, after spending too much time in jail and after the death of his mother, had decided to distance himself from a life of crime and instead find a job working twelve hours, just to get by, giving up on any bigger dreams. Mauro had tried to influence Víctor with advice about the old ways, about the importance of respect and the code of honor between criminals that was rapidly disappearing. Mauro remembers vividly that he was asleep with his wife Nadia when the shots woke him. "I said to her, 'Shit, the kids!' Because every time you hear shots it's because some kid is getting into trouble. I got up, pulled on some shorts, and headed that way."

No sooner had he left his place than a little girl who lived round the corner and knew he was inseparable from Víctor—even though by then he was going straight—said to him the phrase so often repeated that morning:

"I think they've killed Frente."

Mauro ran to the entrance of the San Francisco slum. A cop stopped him: "You can't go through."

Mauro charged on without looking back. The policeman called after him, but Mauro carried on anyway.

"I'm talking to you—hey you, you can't go through!"

"Of course I can!" said Mauro. "I'm on my way home—of course I can go through, there's no tape or anything."

For a few minutes he thought Frente might have escaped, telling Laura,

"The son of a bitch got away!" He climbed onto the roof to make sure. From up there he could see Luis's body protruding from the door of the shack. He was lying still, playing dead for fear that the cops would finish him off. Mauro asked for a camera, and one appeared in no time. He snapped a few pictures to record what he suspected the local Buenos Aires police, the Bonaerense, would hide. He was afraid Víctor was wounded and, with him being a marked man, they would let him bleed to death without any medical assistance. That was why he threatened to rip the roof off the shack if the police didn't get Frente out of there.

Eventually, Luis couldn't stop his legs from beginning to tremble, and one of the officers noticed.

"Hey, watch out—this one's alive!"

Laura saw them take Luis away on a stretcher, his head bloody from the bullet that had grazed his skull. Chaías managed to get close to him. Luis was crying.

"Frente, check on Frente," he managed to say before they loaded him into the ambulance.

Laura panicked a few minutes later when the remaining ambulance left empty.

"Sir, what about the other boy?" she asked one of the officers, afraid of the answer.

"He's inside, it's just that he's fine," the cop lied.

"So why did one of the ambulances leave?"

"Because he's fine, lady," snapped the policeman.

AMONG THOSE PUSHING to see what was going on was Matilde, Frente's closest confidante, a staunch ally when it came to providing cover after a heist. She was a *cartonera* (scrap collector) and mother of Javier, Manuel, and Simon Miranda, Frente's best friends—the kids he had started out with on the road to crime at the age of thirteen. Matilde had managed to slip all the way to the door of the shack and was shouting to Mauro, still making a scene on the roof. She was pretty sure they had killed Frente when she heard Mauro's questions and the evasive replies from a man in a white smock who went into the shack holding a pair of latex gloves.

"What's happening with the kid? Why don't you bring him out?" asked Mauro.

"We'll see in just a minute," the paramedic said evasively.

"Tell me the truth, tell me if he's dead."

"I can't tell you anything," the man cut him off.

"Tell me the truth, man, it's all right. He's dead, isn't he?"

The paramedic didn't say another word, but as he came out of the shack, he lowered his eyes slowly in confirmation.

Víctor's older brother Pato was working a twelve-hour shift at the supermarket where he was a supervisor, and his sister Graciana was married and had gone to live in Pacheco. If no relative turned up, the police would keep holding Víctor in Doña Inés Vera's shack.

"Go get his mom, she's working in the San Cayetano de Carupá supermarket," one kid suggested.

Laura and Chaías set off in a cab. But Sabina was at the Virreyes branch. They returned to the slum. Crowds of people were still piling around the shack. Other neighbors rushed to Virreyes to find her. When they reached Sabina, they told her:

"Come with us, Sabina, there's trouble with the cops!"

"Ah, let them take the bastard, serves him right. I'm not going anywhere," Sabina countered, resisting as always her youngest son's passion for stealing, happy to have him put away in the hope that being locked up in a juvenile institution would turn him into a studious and exemplary teenager.

"Come with us—he's inside a house—come!"

They managed to convince her. Sabina thought: "He's taken someone hostage and he's waiting for me to arrive to give himself up, but before that I'm going to beat the crap out of him . . ." It didn't occur to her that her son had died until the car turned into Quirno Costa Street and from the far side of the empty field she could see a TV crew from Crónica and a helicopter hovering over the crowd. "When I saw the swarm of people and police, my legs shook."

She stepped out of the cab and heard them shouting:

"His mom is coming! His mom is coming!"

She crossed the open field in despair, and people stepped back all down the length of the alley to let her through. It was at that moment that Matilde joined her as her faithful bodyguard, an expert in speaking up for her kids and fighting the police every time they got arrested. Together they arrived at the wall of cops guarding access to the shack. Her mouth set in a tight line, Sabina said, "I'm his mother," and went in.

AT THAT VERY moment, María, Frente's ex-girlfriend, was walking, propped up by her mother, toward the field that borders San Francisco on one side and the 25 de Mayo on the other. The first thing she saw was the thin silhouette of her boyfriend Chaías jumping up and down and shouting in the middle of the field. "Everyone was shouting, I felt giddy all of a sudden, I couldn't see or understand anything. I was really nervous, I was trembling, scared stiff though I wasn't sure of what—not until I reached the door of the shack, because everyone was letting me through, and I saw Sabina."

Sabina Sotello was trying to stay calm, wanting to believe despite everything that the little scoundrel had taken hostages. She asked, trying to appear composed:

"Where's my son?"

The deputy inspector in charge of the operation, a short-haired policewoman, looked at her but didn't want to answer.

"I'm his mother," said Sabina, giving her every reason in the world to reply. Sabina looked all around for Víctor's face but couldn't spot him. "I thought I was going to find him standing there or something and this woman wasn't telling me what was going on, so I lost it." Sabina grabbed the cop by her uniform's collar and pushed her against the small wardrobe that stood in the six-by-six-foot room.

"Where's my son?"

"Calm down, calm down."

"Where is my son?!"

"Calm down, take it easy."

Sabina would not have hesitated to strangle the woman if she didn't talk. She wouldn't take her hands off her until they explained what had happened to Víctor. It was then that she heard the clicking of a typewriter on a small table. "And when you hear that, you sort of know, don't you? When they start typing..."

The man was typing out a legal report on the events that had led to the death of Víctor Manuel Vital that February morning.

The report bore an address: number 57, on the corner of General Pinto Street and French Street. There, at his own front door, Víctor had handed to Gastón, Chaías's older brother, for safekeeping the chains, bracelets, and gold rings that he always wore to show off his status. Then he left, ready to "work," to meet another couple of teens with whom he often carried out robberies: Coqui and Luisito, both also seventeen, from another shantytown with a Catholic name, Santa Rita. These two, as well as two brothers who were the sons of a thug known as Banana, would become famous some time after Víctor's death for one of the first televised hostage takings. They had wanted to rob a family and, instead of leaving in a hurry, got distracted by the sheer amount of luxury goods they found in the chalet in Villa Adelina. Something similar had happened on that February 6 when Victor and his gang took too long to hold up a carpenter's shop just eight blocks from the corner of French and Pintos.

Gastón had tried to talk him out of it: he shouldn't go, the place had a mule (their slang for a private security guard), others had already tried it and failed. Víctor didn't want to believe him. In less than ten minutes, they were pointing a gun at the owner of the furniture factory. In fifteen, they ran out of the place, bad luck on their heels. The two police cars patrolling nearby received a radio alert about the holdup: "Three unidentified males, apparently minors, heading toward Villa 25," they heard. In Unit 12179 rode Sergeant Héctor Eusebio Sosa, alias "Paraguayo," and officers Gabriel Arroyo and Juan Gómez. In Unit 12129 were Corporal Ricardo Rodríguez and Jorgelina Massoni, whose tough-guy attitude had earned her the nickname Little Rambo. The police sirens could be heard coming ever closer. Víctor was in front: he was used to running away. Lately, he hadn't even been able to stand still on a street corner: just being there was enough for him to get arrested. Behind him flew Coqui and Luisito.

"I can't keep going. I can't!" they heard Coqui complain, as he fell behind the other two, his lungs ruined from glue sniffing. While laughing at their straggling friend, Frente and Luis ran into the first alley in the San Francisco slum. Alicia del Castillo, a generously proportioned neighbor, was walking along the path with her two-year-old daughter on one side and a bag of bread on the other. Frente grabbed her by the shoulders with both hands to move her aside. He didn't have the gun on him anymore. They quickly "slipped a shack," as the kids call taking refuge in the first friendly shelter. The woman who let them in to take cover, Doña Inés Vera, stood in the doorway as though just passing the time of day while the boys slid under the table like they were playing hide and seek.

But the police had seen them go in. They didn't even speak to Doña Inés, simply grabbing her by the hair and pushing their way through the doorway. The boys were waiting, unarmed: Luisito told me they gave the guns to Doña Inés, who tossed them behind a wardrobe. They got rid of them so that they could negotiate without a possessions charge in case they had to turn themselves in. The same with the money: Doña Inés hid it under a mattress, and the police found it, although there's nothing about it in the official report.

Crouching beneath the table, Frente put his index finger to his lips: "Shhh... be quiet and we might get away with it...," he whispered, as they saw the policewoman and two male cops enter the shack, pointing their guns. Sergeant Héctor Eusebio Sosa, Paraguayo, was in the lead, with his nine-millimeter pistol. He kicked the table with one steel-tipped boot, sending it flying into a corner. Víctor managed to shout:

"Don't shoot, we surrender!"

Luis says that the two then stammered a repeated "no": "No, no, no"; a "no" meaning that they couldn't believe they would be shot down. "We just covered our heads and said, 'no, no,' like when parents hit you when you're a kid," Luisito told me in a wing of Ezeiza jail on the day he turned twenty-one, doing time for the robberies he continued to commit after Frente's death, excited to be remembering old times after such a long while.

He described the final scene in a rush: in the cramped atmosphere of that miserable six-by-six-foot shack, five shots rang out at point-blank range. Luis realized they were being executed; as if propelled by a spring, he leapt toward the door. A bullet grazed his skull. He landed with his body half out of the shack, having made it just a few feet into the alley. Then he passed out. Frente tried to protect himself by putting his hands in front of his face as if he were blocking out an unwelcome ray of light. Luisito came to a few minutes later, but he remained still as a stone, playing dead.

Frente died almost the moment the police bullets tore into his face. The investigators noted five bullet holes in Víctor Manuel Vital, but there were only four shots. One of them went through the hand he threw up to try to protect himself and entered through his cheekbone. Another penetrated his cheek. The last two struck his shoulder. In the court case, "Paraguayo" Sosa declared that Víctor had died on his feet with a gun in his hand. But at the prosecutor's request, María del Carmen Verdú, the Supreme Court's forensic expert, carried out additional research during the trial. The specialists were asked to determine, given the trajectories of the bullets, how high the barrel of the gun must have been for them to have landed where they did. Accounting for the size of the room and the arrangement of the furniture, if the events had taken place the way Sosa said, he would have to have fired his gun from five feet five inches above the victim. This means that, to have killed Frente the way he described it in court, Sosa would have to have been at least ten feet eight inches tall.

THE POLICEWOMAN, RAISED six inches from the ground by the strength of the woman whose hands were around her neck and going red from the pressure of strangulation, finally admitted to Sabina:

"Your son is dead. He's in there. Don't touch him."

Víctor lay on the dirt floor, the wide, clear forehead that earned him his nickname bathed in a pool of blood, right under the table where the official report of his death was being typed.

Sabina let out a cry of pain. Her arrival at the scene had brought on a silence broken only by the sound of the helicopter hovering above the crowd. Her scream and the sobbing that followed were enough for those waiting outside to lose all hope: a cop had gunned down Víctor Manuel Vital, alias Frente, the best-loved thief in the northern slums of Greater Buenos Aires. He was seventeen years old, and for the past four years he had lived by stealing, but with a different approach to that of other thieves, an approach that earned him his saintly reputation: he shared what he stole with the people of the slum—friends, mothers, girlfriends, men who were out of work, children.

"I KNEW EVERYONE loved him, but I didn't realize there would be such a reaction—even an eighty-year-old lady started throwing stones," Laura tells me. That's how the legend began; it exploded as only battles do. Like a sign from above, they say in the slum, the sky suddenly darkened, black clouds closing in until the slum seemed plunged into night. And it began to rain. The storm stirred violently above the indignant mob. In the downpour, the residents of San Francisco, 25 de Mayo, and La Esperanza fought the police. The news of Frente Vital's death raced through the nearby slums as only bad news can. People came from Santa Rita, from Alvear Bajo, from Detalle. Within half an hour there were nearly a thousand people gathered around the dead teen and 150 cops itching to jump into action. Assault vehicles arrived, the Infantry, the Special Operations Group, the rabid dogs of the provincial police, and still more police with shotguns.

When the shooting started, Laura managed to get close to her friend and finally took refuge in one of the shacks close to where Frente was killed. "There was a crack in the wall and I could see how they took him out and how the sons of bitches laughed and gloated over what they had done. The cops carried him out uncovered, as if displaying him to the world. They didn't show him any respect. I saw him, I saw the sneakers with their big *V* marked on the soles." That was the mark Víctor himself had made, the same

V that his followers now draw on the peeling walls of the slum, alongside the five points that mean "death to the cops."

These are the same five points that Víctor's friends, whom I met as I began to penetrate deeper into the slum, have tattooed in various places on their bodies. Those five marks, each usually about the size of a mole, represent a policeman surrounded by four gang members: one, the cop, in the center, the others surrounding him, equidistant like the corners of a square.

The tattoo indicates that the thief wearing it at some point found himself surrounded by the local cops and that ever since he has been challenging himself to exact revenge: the promise of the five tattooed dots is that the trap will one day be reversed. The picture implies that, in the next encounter, the fatal outcome will be that of the uniformed enemy, cornered now by the force of four thieves seeking revenge. That's why—for the police—this is the unmistakable sign of a criminal record and enough to make anyone with the tattoo a suspect and a likely candidate for a prison cell.

There are five huge dots, as big as casino chips, inked on the back of Matilde's youngest, Simon, just below some tombstones, a dragon, and a skull. Javier, his eldest brother, carries the same mark on his bulging right bicep. Manuel, the middle brother, has them tattooed on his hand. And Facundo, the fourth member of what was a precarious gang, a sort of brother to the rest of them and, above all, a close friend of Frente's, had them done on his left shoulder blade the first time he was held in a police station, at the age of fifteen. Hatred for cops may be the strongest bond between the teens who live by stealing. In their history of loss and humiliation, every young thief has a friend who has been gunned down by the police. For these kids, the death of a friend is one of those incurable wounds that you learn to live with: they are worshipped, cared for, relived in some kind of ritual, and the wound they leave behind is stitched up with memories and tears. As if destiny had wanted to spare them the hollow moment of the wake and funeral of someone they loved, all three of the boys were behind bars the day the cops killed their idol.

The evening before, Simon had a chance to speak to Víctor for the last time: Simon called from the pay phone the kids have access to in Agote, the juvenile institute. "We joked around for a while, just chatting—a bit of this, bit of that. And at one point he said to me:

"'Dude, tomorrow I'm going to send you some stuff. A T-shirt, some shorts...'

"'Nah, it's all good, man. What're you talking about?'

"'Hey, you know we're best friends, don't you?'

"'Everything's great, man. It's all good.'"

They hung up laughing and teasing the way teens do, going from testing each other's smarts with verbal sparring to expressing affection in a roundabout way, hidden beneath loyalty or respect.

That night, Simon fell asleep thinking once again about the day he'd be back on the streets. He missed being in the slum, returning home after an "event," his pockets stuffed with banknotes, and then losing himself in Tropitango, or Metropolis, another nightclub downtown.

The next day, he placed a collect call to his friend Laura's place. At the far end of the line he heard the bewilderment left by death, the anguish that precedes having to share a terrible piece of news. Laura was with Mariela, her friend at the time.

"No, you tell him," Simon heard.

"No, you do it . . . ," came down the line.

"What's going on?" he nearly shouted in the silence of the Agote jail.

". . ."

"What do you have to say to me, guys?"

". . ."

"Hey, get your shit together!"

"They killed Frente."

"When?!"

"Just now."

"You're crazy. I just talked to him yesterday!"

Laura started sobbing, and then he had to believe her. He didn't even need to hear the details. He knew Víctor Vital was a marked man for the San Isidro police. All he could do at that moment was hang up, go back to his cell, shut himself even farther in his seclusion, and cry alone.

He rolled a huge joint using all the weed he had, lit it, and breathed in deeply. Without exhaling, he put some music that Frente used to listen to on the CD player he'd been given. First, cumbia from Colombia, then contract killers' cumbia, then the Mexican band Cañaveral. Finally, a song that Frente listened to religiously.

Cuando me muera quiero que me toquen cumbia / y que no me recen cuando suenen los tambores / y que no me lloren porque me pongo muy triste / no quiero coronas ni caritas tristes / solo quiero cumbia para divertirme. (Dance for me when I die / don't pray for me when the drums sound / and don't cry for me, it'll make me too sad / I don't want wreaths or mournful faces / I just want cumbia and to have a good time.)

FACUNDO HAD ALSO been jailed some time before Frente's murder. He was caught after a heist with Chaías, when a police patrol crossed their path as they were returning to the slum, whistling softly after holding up a bakery. Chaías lagged behind a couple of minutes because he wanted to pay off a debt he owed nearby before spending the rest on pills. Facundo ended up inside the Monsignor Emilio Ogñenovich Institution in Mercedes, a rehabilitation center for addicts that later became known for abusing and torturing the teens held there. He, too, found out about Frente's murder that day.

"It was a disaster. He was beside himself. He started breaking stuff and fought the guards. He even tried to jump the barbwire, wanting to escape. They beat him up, bad. Afterward, he was still having problems—we went to visit, and he was struggling. They drugged him up, giving him shots, and he was shaking—he was so full of stuff. He was hurt, with wounds everywhere, cuts around his mouth, his eyebrow split, his whole body torn up from the barbwire because they pulled him down by his pant legs, dragging him through the spikes. From there they took him to a community for addicts in Florencio Varela. He got better there, he was treated by psychologists." This was what I was told one afternoon by his grandmother, one of the *mai umbanda* in the hood.[2] It was through Facundo that Luis met Frente, and in turn, through Luis that Frente got to know Coqui, the other member of Los Bananita, the guys he went out to steal with for the last time.

THAT FEBRUARY 6, Manuel was being held in San Fernando's First Precinct for his latest failed robbery. "I was with the other guys in the cell watching *Saturday Forever* on Channel 2. When the ads came on, we started channel surfing. Suddenly on Crónica TV there was a banner: 'Breaking News. San Fernando.'"

"Hold on, man, I live there," Manuel stopped the guy with the remote control to the TV that hung outside the cell.

He recognized the streets, the shacks, the open field. And he watched as they took out a stretcher with a body on it. Although the camera was far away, he thought he recognized the clothes his friend was wearing.

---

2 *Mai umbanda* are religious leaders of Umbanda, a spiritual practice stemming from African religions and originating in Brazil. Female priests are *mai* (mother), and male priests are *pai* (father).—Trans.

"I hope to God it's not, but that looks like Frente," he said to his friends in the cell.

His cell mates were two other teens from his hood and another from Boulogne who had also done time with Frente. They all fell silent. "At the end, when they had him nearly inside the ambulance, I recognized the *V* on his soles. I was sure he was dead, the way they were carrying him. After that there were a lot of gunshots from the cops and stones thrown by the people in the slum. I couldn't believe it. It was Crónica TV live, and you could see everyone. I had gone down a month earlier, and I was really pissed that I wasn't there with him, because if we'd been together, maybe it wouldn't have happened that way. I was in bad shape in that moment. I wanted to die, nothing mattered after that. They said they wasted a guard, beat him up badly, that it was an intense fight."

Women were kicking cop cars, spitting at the Special Operations Group. The police had to form a line, and the rioters charged it time and again. One of the cops got hit in the leg; another one had his collarbone smashed with a stick. Sabina will never forget seeing Matilde, the mother of Manuel, Simon, and Javier, who had always been so distant, so on the side of the gang members—something she herself had always refused to be, choosing instead to disdainfully condemn her son's illegal activities. She remembers her running in the rain during all the shooting, mud up to her knees, losing her flip-flops in the fight—like María, who in the heat of battle left hers drowned in the mud.

THE VIOLENCE WAS so intense that Sabina Sotello had to snap out of her stupor, take a deep breath, and think about what she could do to calm the vengeful fury over her son's death. She feared the police might fire real bullets and was afraid that, if the clash continued, people would bring out the weapons they had hidden in the nearby slums because of the rumors of a police raid planned for that weekend. Revenge was at hand for the enraged relatives, as sticks and stones continued to fly at the cops and their see-through shields. "I thought someone else was going to get killed, and I had to do something." Sabina crossed the alley and spoke to the crowd.

"Please listen to me. Let's end this before there is another victim, let's stop so these sons of bitches will leave!" she said.

Slowly, the combatants' fury calmed, and the afternoon was given over to mourning. "To top it all off, it rained so hard the rain was like tears," said dark, lanky Chaías. As the deluge pelted down, he walked along brandishing an enormous red umbrella against the wind. It looked as though it had been taken from a family beach on the coast, a surreal Japanese image in the midst of all this misery.

Sabina went back to the shack where the public prosecutor and court officials were waiting for a signal to leave the slum, terrified at the real possibility they could be lynched. "In the end, they left huddled together like wet chickens, holding on to my arm and Matilde's," Sabina told me more than once over the course of our unhurried conversations as she accompanied me on the long journey to reconstruct this death, a journey with no specific end date.

Matilde did not leave Sabina's side after that, as if the bullets had hit one of her own sons. In some sense, Víctor had been like a son to her throughout those years of robberies and violence. The two women went together to the police station to go through the bureaucratic paperwork that the relatives of kids who are shot down always have to face. They spent five hours at the local precinct until they were told that it would take some time for the body to be handed over. Laughing tenderly, Sabina often recalls how Matilde, ashamed of her bare feet after losing her flip-flops, sat on a bench trying to conceal them by putting one on top of the other under the seat, hiding them like a little girl.

On the evening after the death, Manuel spoke with his mother on the phone from his cell at the police station; he begged her to request permission for him to be at the wake, a transfer judges often grant inmates when a close relative dies. But although Manuel and Simon were granted leave, neither Sabina nor Matilde allowed them to go. To this day, Manuel and Simon feel hurt that they were left out of that farewell ceremony, but the atmosphere in the vigil was so charged that Matilde and Sabina thought it would be too dangerous. The weapons that had disappeared from the hood owing to fears of a raid came back out again as soon as Frente was murdered. "I never saw so many guns in one place," Sabina told me regarding the contents of her son's friends' pockets. If the brothers were to be transferred to the house on French and General Pinto where Víctor's body was laid out, it had to be done by police from the First Precinct. This was where Rambito and Sosa were stationed, and everybody saw them as accomplices in the unjust death, just as guilty as the person who pulled the trigger.

The police, too, were still enraged after the fiasco that Saturday. The resentment of the officers of San Fernando's First Precinct didn't end with that day's violence. That was where Manuel was being held when everything went down. "As soon as they killed him, they came to gloat at me, and then all hell broke loose. I fought with them and threw a thermos of boiling water at one cop. The guys fought them with me, but then the cops wanted to take me out on my own to beat me up. They took me to the Boulogne precinct and only brought me back to the Number One later. I sat there, doing nothing, just thinking. I wanted to die. I got the urge to write. I couldn't stop remembering."

IT RAINED ALL that day and night. But despite the stormy weather, from the moment of his death there were always mourners waiting for Frente's body at the door to number 57 Pinto Street. "We had to wait for three days for them to hand him over to us. They wanted to let me have a wake for two or three hours. I told them to go to hell. I told them I was going to keep a vigil for as long as I wanted, as long as I felt he deserved. I argued with them. I said that at that moment, they were my employees, that I was paying their wages and that they were going to do what I said. We held the wake here because people sometimes don't have enough for bus fare," Sabina tells me, in the same room where Víctor's body was laid out. "This place was full of people, people I had never seen before in my life, they came from all over."

It became a crowded site of pilgrimage. That block on French Street between Pinto and Ituizangó filled up with kids who collected in groups on the street corners, like they so often do in the northern slums of Buenos Aires. "After a while, the kids who came round started to collect money to buy wreaths," I was told by Chaías, who spent the night there. "Whenever something like that happens, someone starts collecting to buy the deceased the wreaths they deserve." Many of them were armed. Some stood on a corner and started firing shots in the air as remembrance in the middle of the prayers, and Pato, Víctor's older brother, had to impose order and tell the guys to cool it. The patrol cars from the First Precinct never stopped prowling around the house all through the twenty-four hours of that last farewell. Every once in a while they would sound their sirens to make their presence felt. Sabina tried to make sure that nobody reacted to the provocation. Chaías says they were so heavily armed they could have stood in front of a police car and destroyed it if each of the avenging teens had fired a clip into it. They held off until the following morning, Tuesday, when at nearly nine o'clock they took the coffin out of the kitchen and put it into the hearse.

That was when they could control themselves no longer. A chaotic volley of shots fired into the air was their good-bye to Víctor Manuel Vital, Frente. And those shots began to transform his death into a consecration; in his absence, the possibility of salvation.

There were so many people that it took two buses and a truck with a trailer to carry the whole procession. The line of cars, all the cabs of the area as well as those stolen that weekend, wound its way all around the outside of the 25 de Mayo slum.

All along Quirno Costa Street on the edge of the empty lot, a line of teens emptied clips, shooting into the dried-up mud. "We left here and went round the places where he used to hang out. When the funeral procession appeared in front of the slum, shots rang out as if it were Christmas. That was Víctor's farewell," Sabina remembers proudly. He was buried with the colors of Boca Juniors and Tigre's soccer teams covering his coffin. Among the dozens of wreaths, there was one exactly like what he'd asked for during those last months when he was being harassed by the police: "If they get me, make me a wreath in Boca's colors," he had said, as if joking about a preordained future.

2

Two years had passed since I first set foot in the "slum." That's what I called that seemingly impregnable territory from the start, although in fact the characters in this story crisscross three slums. "The slum," "Tomorrow I'm going to the slum," "I'm having a barbecue at the slum," "I have a birthday to go to at the slum," "This Sunday there's a kid expecting me at the slum." At first, the slum was a tiny territory, limited to the few square yards in which I felt free to move about. The bewilderment of an outsider getting to know the characters and the place, the language, the codes, incomprehensible to begin with; the difficulty of the first conversations—all this gradually gave way to a kind of familiarity, the sense of belonging you feel when you walk down a block and exchange greetings with people, chatting with some about the weather or asking others what the kids are up to—kids who are always so hard to pin down, who have no schedule but instead simply breathe in the present moment as deeply as they can, the actual moment they are in, never allowing any new activity or commitment to bring it to a close by imposing the future on it.

When I first met Sabina Sotello, I never imagined I would still be visiting her so long afterward, that we would speak on the phone so often, and that she would, like a worried mom, chide me if I stayed away for too long. Nor could I foresee that in the end, she would be the one guiding me, without my knowing it, into the secrets of the shantytowns where Frente was king—accompanying me with her energy and her maternal presence into shacks I had never before been allowed to enter. It was almost a month before July 29, Víctor Vital's birthday, a date on which she, family, and friends organized a giant festival for the local kids with hot chocolate, games, and races on skateboards made from wooden planks supplied by her eldest son, who works at a sawmill. She was waiting for me at the entrance to a supermarket in San Isidro in her security guard uniform. Yes, Sabina, the mother of the young thief who was killed and canonized, had for some time been earning a living in a job deliberately chosen as the exact opposite of her son's illegal activities.

There was a moment, she told me in the cab taking us from the busy asphalt of the Pan-American Highway to the slum, when she didn't know anymore how to stop him, to convince him to give up his criminal ways. That's when she signed up to train as a security guard. Víctor saw it as a joke, a feature that added color to his choice of cunningly relieving others of their cash. "Ha, the mother is a guard, and the kid a thief!" he said when she told him. "So let's see when you case a joint for me, Sotello," he teased. To "case a joint" is to check out the details of a place that a person later intends to burglarize.

Before becoming a guard, Sabina had struggled for years and made every effort to achieve some sort of economic stability so she could give her kids the things she never had herself. Growing up in a shack near the village of Las Palmas in Chaco, a province in northern Argentina, Sabina and her two brothers had to walk barefoot several miles every morning to get to school. They lived on a small plot of dry land, "like the poorest of the poor." She was fourteen when she fell in love with a policeman, a forbidden first love. Her father, a sugar-mill worker, hated uniforms. "When he found out I was pregnant, he beat me until I bled with one of those whips they use to herd cattle. I was writhing like a snake from the pain. That's why I detest my old man."

The policeman wanted them to live together and to recognize him as the child's father, but Sabina's family was so incensed, she decided to go it alone. After the baby was born, she heard that her father wanted to register the baby as his own, so she got up at dawn and went to the nearest town, where she named the baby Julio César and registered him as her son. When she returned, her parents beat her again. She had to wait a year before her older brother, who had left for Buenos Aires, sent her the money for bus fare so she could get away.

She arrived in San Fernando, on the outskirts of Buenos Aires, to work as a live-in maid for a wealthy family. There, she met the woman who would become a mother figure to her for the rest of her life. "In that house worked a woman who I adopted as my real mother, Odulia Medina. She took a liking to me, and since I didn't have anyone, she started inviting me over when I had the day off. In the hood, they're so nosy that she told everyone I was her husband's daughter from a previous marriage. I started to call him Dad and her Mom. They were so good to me that I ended up living with them, in a shack just around the corner from here."

She fell in love again, with someone who seemed like a good man and who became the father of her second child, but things ended up even worse than before. They bought some land in José C. Paz and went to live there together. Her son Pato was two years old when she escaped from this man and his beatings and went back to her adoptive parents' house. Later on, she gave love another shot with a third man. She moved in with her new in-laws and got pregnant with Graciana, but that relationship didn't last either. By this time, she had taken a photography course and could make a living photographing school portraits, birthday parties, weddings, and some Peronist political campaigns. Her new partner was a lathe operator who made good money but spent it on alcohol and partying: he'd go off on Friday and reappear on Monday. That was when Víctor arrived.

Sabina put up with the situation until the death of her mother-in-law, who had been her only protection against the father of her newest child. She had opened a joint bank account with him and one day found the balance was zero, all gone on women and booze. The story ended at lunchtime one day when she was making pasta. A fight broke out, and he put a gun to her head in front of the kids. After that, he began to do target practice with a plaster statue of Christ that she venerated by lighting candles.

She had gotten to know people while taking photos, among them a political organizer with contacts in the Otero police station. She told him what had happened. "And so they arrested his ass. And we made the most of it, taking the opportunity to escape. We put everything in a truck and came to the slum. That's when I bought the shack that is now this house, and we settled in," she reminisced one day at the bar on the corner of the San Fernando hospital after visiting one of the slum kids who was close to death in intensive care.

Víctor Vital hardly ever lived with his father. He knew him only because of the hell he raised every now and then at the door to their house, harassing Sabina and threatening her, saying he was going to kill her. It was his mother who worked herself to death to get him his Adidas sneakers and the best school uniform. But she herself admits that, since she had to work, she wasn't able to control him. "Because it was just us again, I was never at home. I had to work all the time just to make sure he was fed. And Víctor got out of hand. Without me noticing, he started taking drugs, and after that there was no way to stop him. When he was thirteen, the police reports began: stolen bicycles, sneakers—stupid things like that—but still not what I expected of him. All I wanted was for him to study." Sabina told me how she then signed him up for a computer course near the San Fernando train station. He would leave at the right time every day, with his folder under his arm, but then he would drop it at a friend's house and go out on the street; it was the perfect cover. "I asked to see what he did, and he always said he'd forgotten his work at school. Then one day I went to speak to the teacher, and she told me he'd never been there."

Frente began to go off the sacred path his mother had imagined for him when he was twelve years old and still in seventh grade. He found school unbearably boring; the street was dizzying, but it called to him. One of his first tricks was to pretend that he was too sick for school. Taking advantage of a fall while he was playing around, he pretended he had broken his arm. That was when Manuel met him for the first time. "He was beginning to break loose and get together with us. I remember he had his arm in a cast, but he had put it on himself just so he didn't have to go to school. We knew it was a lie and thought it was hilarious. Afterward, when his mom took him to the doctor, she found out. That was around the time when we first got to know him. We'd go together to the fancy Belgrano neighborhood with my brothers, Javier and Simon, and began to steal down there. Back then we were into stealing the expensive bikes that were popular—we'd sell them for two hundred pesos."

Manuel has fond memories of those bikes that were everywhere among the middle class during the 1990s. The ones you could lift with a finger—aerodynamic, lightweight metal bikes with dozens of gears; flying bicycles of the consumerist decade under President Carlos Menem that the San Fernando kids carried away to a place not too far from their home.

Manuel is the middle child of the Miranda family: one of Matilde's children, one of Víctor's best friends, and a great thief. It took me a few months of waiting before I got a chance to meet him, because when I first arrived at the slum he was doing time in the Olmos jail for armed robbery. His look in some of the photos his mother showed me, a mixture of resentment and childish sweetness, with his slim build and a seriousness that seemed slightly put on—the eyebrows arched in a teen's tough-guy imitation—along with the anecdotes Sabina told me about his tight friendship with Victor, kept me eagerly awaiting his release. It was the same with my wait for permission to see Simon, his younger brother, who was locked up in the almost inaccessible Instituto Almafuerte. In the tumultuous days of December 2001,[1] we were sure Manuel would be out on New Year's Day 2002. But a bad behavior report and postponed paperwork dashed our hopes—his mother's, his brother's, and mine. It was not until March, after a year and eight months, that he saw the horizon of the pampas, that vast expanse of empty land that floods prisoners' eyes when they emerge from the Olmos jail.

I finally met him in his older sister Estela's dark kitchen. She's the mother of four innocent-looking children who were fighting over the TV remote to make sure there was always an action movie on. Manuel seemed calm, very much at home; he knew I had been wanting to interview him for a long time. Honestly, I was a bit nervous. I wondered what I could do to seem like a hardened journalist at home in the slum, with all the respect needed to win over this kid newly back on the streets. We drank some beer. It took three quick glasses for me to drown my initial timidity. We started talking about his childhood. He was eight when he first hit the streets. "I just wandered around. I sold cleaning cloths with a friend," he told me while his nephews and nieces dangled from his arms and the youngest sat on his knee. His first confessions got me used to listening, to paying special attention to his prison slang with its short, swallowed sentences. Of the three brothers whom I would eventually meet, Manuel was the most withdrawn. Somehow he was able to quell my constant urge to ask questions, keeping it hidden beneath small talk about the weather or short silences, during which I watched as his sharp features slowly softened around his deep green eyes. In a strange way, I felt I learned something from his reticence, respecting the minutes that could stretch between an observation of mine and a tepid reaction from him, between an evil look and a chuckle at a dirty joke.

The first time Manuel went to prison with Frente, it was because of a mechanical problem. Víctor's motorcycle, an XR100 that Sabina had bought for him by saving up many hours of her overtime pay as a security guard, broke

---

[1] In December 2001, Argentina experienced a run on the banks, five presidents in two weeks, and numerous protests that left dozens dead or injured.—Trans.

down after he and Manuel held up an Esso gas station in Martínez. That afternoon, Manuel was wearing a Boca football top and shorts. He says that he didn't have to shoot: he just lifted his shirt and revealed the gun tucked into his waistband before muttering to his victim, "Gimme the money or you die."

They got stranded near the San Isidro racetrack and had to drag the motorbike to a garage to be repaired. When it was ready, Manuel paid with a bag of freshly stolen coins, practically still warm from the previous owners. "Keep the change," he said to the nosy but grateful mechanic. They hadn't gone ten blocks when they were surrounded by half a dozen police cars. The cops were on their way to a raid at a sports store they'd gotten a tip about. Manuel had been back on the streets for a month; he had come from the worst experience of his life, the Almafuerte juvenile detention center. This time he ended up in Balneario precinct, in a cell where he had to listen in silence to Sabina's recriminations and advice for the whole of her first visit. Like Matilde, Frente's mom saw the friendship between the two boys as the source of all the evils that led them astray. From then on, they were forbidden to spend time together. They began keeping their friendship and criminal activities under wraps, coming up with a system of signals and nods, like in the old tango dances, that could be seen from corner to corner—from Sarratea and French, where the Mirandas lived, to French and Pinto, Frente's place—so that they could set a time and place to meet up.

"If they saw us together around the hood, they thought the worst," Manuel told me as we sat one fall, restlessly watching the sunset. "It's the same way now—even if I'm not out to steal, if they see me wearing something new, they ask if we're off to the city to hold some place up." He told me about the times he and Chaías got dressed up—putting on chinos, dress shirts, leather jackets, good shoes—to visit Buenos Aires. "When we got back they wanted to know where we'd been, if we did anything, how it went." After a while, a thief's bad reputation sticks, even after he gets out of the vicious cycle of crime; but Manuel admits to feeling angry about it now that he no longer steals, now that he's trying to reclaim his life, and his weapons are, at most, just a necessary form of defense for surviving in the hood. In the case of him and Víctor—the cursed couple—Manuel, as the widower, thinks the police and judges labeled them as dangerous and violent way too early, as if they carried it in their blood, as if it were an incurable, congenital disease. "After they caught us the first time, none of them wanted to see us together. Even the cops would say that to our mothers—they told them that we were getting arrested because we hung out together, that if we weren't together, we wouldn't be in this mess. It was like, 'Look who he's hanging with. We're handing him back, but we don't want to see him around here again.' That's what they said, and the moms believed them, until, thankfully, one day they didn't buy it anymore."

They only had to look at each other, and the street became a vast expanse of possibilities. One day Frente's motorcycle was impounded for good by the cops after Sabina refused to go and claim it yet again, hoping that, without wheels, Víctor would stop stealing. The alternative was his brother's motorcycle—but they had to swear by the Virgin and their mother that they would not use it for anything illegal—or a car that belonged to Victor's brother-in-law, who was more on their side. "Sometimes, when he managed to get hold of some wheels, he'd say, 'I'll wait for you around the corner.' We'd stop half a block away from a place, and he'd walk into the joint, or maybe behind me, all cool, flash the gun, bang, bang, get out, foot down on the pedal, and we'd be gone. Everywhere we'd go was like that. Until he bought himself a jeep." Frente was doing well and even saving money, although he was still helping others out when they needed it. With his half-paternalistic, half-mocking style, cool but with a generosity that kept people from resenting him for his powerful ego, Frente was capable of donating everything in his pockets for the worst or the best of causes. He made no moral distinction with his handouts, his daily contributions toward the needs of others, or his intended gifts. People in the slums still recall that Frente gave with ease and detachment as if he were a wastefully extravagant kid. He seemed to spend for the sake of spending rather than out of pure generosity. And partying was, of course, the biggest and most flashy way to spend his ill-gotten gains.

For the gang members who want cumbia played when they die, dancing is a funeral ceremony turned into a block party; it is for dedicating everything gained from an outburst of violence verging on death to the madness of the dance floor, to the frantic heartbeats that come only from coke, to the distortion of images, colors, and meanings that comes with the mixing of pills and alcohol. As a tribute to the historical paganism of the slums—what could also be defined as a vitality of the extreme slums, or the extreme vitality of the slums—Frente and his friends like Manuel dedicated much of their takings to the consumption of large jugs of alcohol, and to the swaying mass of four thousand kids who gathered from every corner of the northern slums, brought by buses that ventured into all the poorest nooks and crannies to pick up the crowds willing to travel any distance to see the latest groups onstage at Tropitango. Tropi is that dive on the Pan-American Highway and 202nd Street that has aptly been dubbed "the cathedral of slum cumbia," where the beverage of choice is the "crazy jug"—a mixture of all kinds of alcohol and whatever pills anyone can manage to drop into it. "With two hundred pesos on a Friday . . . Wow! Dance, women, drink, fashion," Manuel remembered fondly. "Sometimes my wallet would be totally stuffed, I couldn't even close it. But when you're generous, you forget about it, you don't care about the money you pull out, you spend it like it's water, like you don't have long to live."

Not dying too soon, surviving on the streets despite risking their lives—this is the kind of thing the kids pray to Frente for. "Before going to work, I kiss the photo I have in a frame with the Tigre team colors," Chaías told me, sitting against a cement wall in the same shadow that reaches the grave of the miracle worker. Chaías—so skinny he looks almost emaciated, hair spiked and always gelled, thick eyebrows, full lips, slow in his movements, eighteen years old and father of two children—is proud that he and Frente had the same style. Frente took great care about his personal aesthetics, using it to set himself apart from the rest, and Chaías tries to preserve that style. He wears loose pants, ironed just right with a perfect crease, an impeccable Lacoste polo shirt, and white Nikes that he had to soak for two days to get clean after the mudfest of the last dance. "People always tell me, 'You really remind me of Frente.' He'd have on his cologne, he'd shower like three times a day. The shorts, the T-shirts, the jeans, the vest, the Nikes." Chaías loves to keep his Nikes clean, jumping over the puddles left by the last rain as if he were a ballerina in a tutu, on tiptoe, so as not to stain his sneakers. He wears two thick gold chains around his neck, a broad bracelet, and a watch on his left wrist that brings to mind the rich kid who must have worn it before it was snatched from him at gunpoint. "I never worked with him, I didn't start stealing until after he died. But every time he saw me, he would invite me along, just like that." Dressed to the nines, they would go and stuff themselves at the Chinese restaurants in the center of San Fernando. "We'd all go in a cab. After dinner we'd play pool and then go clubbing. Sometimes he'd grab me and say, 'Come on Chaías, let's go get some clothes,' and we'd go to a mall."

Chaías is a different kind of thief, in between the generation of young gang members with a code of honor, like Frente, Manuel, or Javier, and those who came after them, who are less well equipped, less careful, and more vulnerable; those who over the past three years have gone out into the streets in desperation and with increasingly less nerve. Manuel himself told me one time, when the three of us were having dinner, that they didn't do robberies with Chaías. "He's just got a different vibe. He's younger, we started out before him. We looked at him and thought, he doesn't cut it." At that table, totally out of it after having spent the day sniffing glue, all Chaías said to explain it was: "Apart from anything else, it was out of respect for my old man." Months later, I would discover, although I already suspected as much, that Chaías's father was a dealer in the slum.

I first met Chaías at Sabina's house. He was sitting with his hands crossed, freshly dressed, slurring his words a bit but making intelligent arguments. He was the one who really introduced me to the legend of Frente, the one who stirred my imagination about the sensitive and cursed kid who had left such a mark. On the one hand, Chaías defended his dead friend and spread the word about him like a banner he refused to put down. He filled me with stories about Víctor's intrinsic goodness and the way he mediated between the most violent and the most fragile in their turf. In every account of what this devotion means, there is a constant comparison between the times before Frente's death and what happened in the slum afterward: the mess, the madness, the lack of respect, the treachery, the stealing—even from your own neighbors and people who have nothing. Though his methods were often questionable, Frente did impose some order in the narrow confines of the shantytown. Chaías remembers him not so much as a thief, but as a sort of monitor in the slum. Without that backing, which allowed Chaías to walk undisturbed through the alleys and streets of the slum, he now lives in fear. "It's not like before. When Frente was around, nobody messed with him. Now everyone wants to pull one over on you—they're nothing, but they think they're hot shit. When he was around, he'd just look at them and say, 'What the hell guys?' or 'Get a grip! This is my hood!'" To make his point, Chaías reproduces one of Frente's dialogues:

"'You're getting ahead of yourself. That's not how you do it, man,' Frente ticked off one guy because he'd kept a gun a neighbor had lent him.

"'No, Frente—stop. Please, man, stop,' the guy tried to defend himself.

"'Get out of here, asshole. I don't want to see you around!'

"And he slapped him round the head," Chaías recounted, describing the foolhardy guy who broke rules as old as the slum, rules that have fallen by the wayside as poverty there has increased exponentially. The kid he threw out only came back to the slum after Frente's death.

Sabina Sotello tells it her way: "Nobody ever came to tell me, Hey, look,

Sabina, your son dissed me, your son is causing trouble, or hit my kid, or whatever. Nobody ever came to complain about him. The only ones who ever turned up were the cops."

Rather than complain about him to his mother, the neighbors were more likely to cover for him. When a bullet severed a tendon in his arm, one woman on the block stitched him up, another gave him a tetanus shot, and all Sabina was told was that he had fallen off his bike. If you walk through the slum, the women will tell you the same story: they'd come home and find Frente there watching TV, hiding from the police. "What are you doing here? Go to your own place," they would say. And he would smile and ask them to be nice and give him money to get a Coke and some takeout. All of them say they succumbed to his charm. Just as his manner drove the local cops crazy. "He was terrible when he was in jail, he drove them up the wall," they all say.

There are certain things his faithful always bring up in Frente's canonization: his generosity with the hauls from his robberies, the respect he inspired through his unrelenting enmity toward the police, and his role as preserver of the slum's unofficial order. And nobody fails to mention a before and after in the slum's existence marked by his death. "He was just a kid when he cut up the bunk bed because we didn't use the top one and gave it to a kid who was sleeping on the floor," explains his mother, the person who most detested and condemned his criminal ways. "Get your dirty money out of here! You know where you can stuff it!" she'd say. That same misbegotten money also pissed off his brother, who put in twelve-hour days as a store manager, when he learned what Frente was up to. "Whenever I caught him stealing, I beat the shit out of him," he says. Still, Pato is proud of him. "Not because he stole, but because of what he did with the money." This difficult relationship with his family explains Víctor's generosity. He had nothing to spend it on: he didn't need to give half to a desperately poor mother, like his friends did. He was always willing to share what he had in his pockets with whoever needed it.

"I remember one night that he didn't get into Tropi because they found rolling paper on him, and he came over," said Chaías. "That evening, we were dressed the same: tan chinos, leather jacket, white shirt, vest. He asked me if I had any money. I had fifteen pesos, he had twelve. So he said, 'Come on let's go eat.' On our way we bumped into a kid who asked him for a peso so he could get something to eat. He gave it to him. We called a cab to go to Sporting, a diner we always went to in San Fernando. The car came, honked, we got in, and the little kid ran alongside to join us. Víctor was cracking up and said, 'Hurry up, hurry.' The kid was desperate, and the car had to go as fast as it could. 'Hurry, hurry,' said Víctor, and left him behind. He was a shit like that sometimes. We went into Sporting looking good, and we got breaded chicken escalopes, beer, and Fanta. Just when we started to eat, I got such a bad toothache I couldn't keep eating. But I still had half of my food left, so Victor asks, 'You want a doggie bag?' I brought it home on a tray. We had a good time that day."

In a hidden alley in the 25 de Mayo slum, the one that Víctor ran down on the morning of his death, I'm talking to Paraná, dyed blond, shorts, freckles, and baseball cap, who tells me about the time they robbed a joint together. It was the two of them, both underage, and one older boy. They held up a supermarket dressed as two schoolkids with their sports coach. They arrived looking tiny, in the white overalls schoolkids in Argentina wear and with books under their arms, ideal for hiding their guns. The older kid wore Adidas sweats. They thought Víctor could pretend to be the teacher and Paraná, the student. They entered playing their roles. Víctor pulled out a .38 and stared the cashiers and customers in the eye. Thanks to a tip from somebody who worked there, they thought there would be twenty thousand pesos in the office. But it didn't work out: the office was closed. They decided to go with what was in the registers. "Stay calm, we'll do our thing and leave. Don't get nervous, nobody will get hurt," Paraná recalls Frente saying to all those present. They left the place looking like students again, with some twenty-three hundred pesos stuffed in the pages of their notebooks. But even that couldn't compare, Paraná admits, with the heist on the delivery truck they hijacked from the dairy company La Serenísima, which was full to the brim with food. Even according to the devotees who now recount his adventures as a thief as if they were rosary bead recitations, this was his best heist.

Sabina walks toward the house of Matilde, the woman who was like a mother to her son, as well as the mother of his best friend and co-conspirator. On the way, she greets everyone she comes across. In the slums, greetings are a sign of respect, as important as your name. And Sabina is important, just like her son was back in the day. Not only is she the woman to go to if you have a problem with the police, because now she works with human rights organizations and relatives of other kids who have been gunned down, but there's also something about her, her smile, that carries a little trace of Víctor even after his death. In the eyes of the world, she is still "Frente's mom." Maybe because of this—in spite of having resisted her youngest son's bad choices—she shows me the legendary La Serenísima truck with a sort of grudging pride. It's one of those refrigerated trucks that goes round each day supplying stores with fresh dairy products. One day the kids—that is, Frente with Manuel and Simon, Matilde's sons—hijacked it, emptied the contents into the kinds of carts used by many slum dwellers who collect cardboard boxes at night, and then doled out the proceeds, the way left-wing guerrillas did during the 1970s. The goods even reached prisons: the best Argentinian cheeses went to satisfy the hunger of prisoners in La Nueva, Devoto, Caseros, Sierra Chica, and Olmos. "Frente was convinced that small kids should have yogurt and not sweets," says Matilde, in her house full of small armchairs that she's picked up on her rounds collecting paper and cardboard on the streets for a living. "When he went to the candy store, they would come up to him and ask him, and he'd buy them stuff. With the truck, the slum was full of dairy products—yogurt, pasteurized milk, things we never could have had before."

It was Chaías who helped me understand how, these days, a person's space in the hood is increasingly limited to their home, and how even crossing some very near and familiar borders could mean death. Settled near the La Esperanza slum, Chaías lives with his father, a younger sister, and an older brother in a shack with a kitchen, a room for him, and another two in the back. Every now and then over the past four years, he's also lived with the mother of his two three-year-old kids, María—Frente's ex-girlfriend who was washing clothes when she heard about the fate of the guy she still loved. "When we got together, we were both fourteen. She had fallen out with Frente when he was in prison. That's when we started seeing each other, and afterward he and I were still friends, we still saw each other. María got pregnant a few weeks after they killed him." They had twins and baptized one of them Víctor Manuel.

At Chaías's place we had several blowouts and parties. Some of us would bring meat for the barbecue, and his dad would fry delicious empanadas. Afterward, with Chaías and the rest of his friends from that part of the slum, we'd move to the corner where we'd kill time on a Sunday or a holiday, with other kids dropping by, teasing passersby, or playing a pickup game that I always watched from the sidelines. There would be a jug with wine and some pills—usually Rohypnol or Artane—that the kids at first would offer me. I only tried the drink once, and it tasted like poison: almost as soon as I drank some, my mind became fuzzy and I was perplexed at how slowly time seemed to be passing.

María would come to the corner with the kids to leave them with Chaías and the rest of the gang for a while. When his children were with him, Chaías never sniffed glue. On my third day in San Fernando, Chaías was using up the last dregs he had in a plastic bag. He was paranoid about two kids staring at him from the entrance to one of the San Francisco alleys as we leaned against a wall opposite, a field where some thieves and a local cop were playing soccer. "Orejita," he warned the youngster who was with him holding another bag to his nose. "Orejita, shit's going down, those guys want a piece of us." They'd recently clashed with the Sapitos, a gang that they call "rats" or "vermin" in the slum—kids so off their heads on pills that they steal from their own neighborhoods. At the time, Chaías had to watch where he went in his ever-shrinking turf. Not only did he have to be prepared for a treacherous attack by the Sapitos, but he also couldn't show his face in the slum where his girlfriend María lived. "It's all fucked up—any move and they stab you in the back. And the cops shoot you from behind as well," Chaías told me. At the time, I didn't realize that what he was saying cloaked his many internal conflicts, which even later, as I got to know him better, I found hard to fully understand.

Among other reasons, Chaías couldn't go to see María because his father-in-law, Chano, her stepdad, hated him. She was dangerous, too, as he explained, a bit out of it from the glue sniffing. "I'm separated from my woman, but we're friends. Not all the time, though, because sometimes she sees me with another girl and gets all worked up and lashes out. She doesn't tell me, she doesn't come up to me and say, 'What the hell! Leave her,' or whatever. She goes and beats the girl up. I don't go to her hood much, so sometimes I don't get to see the kids for a long time, because I could go over there and the guys in the hood over there might give me hell. They sell a lot of drugs over there, they're dealers, and there's no peace between us gangs. You have to risk your life just to feed them. I mean, if you want some coke, who do you pay? Them. And sometimes it's a pain in the ass having to steal for the dealers. There's good people and bad people. Well, the dealers are bad. They're bad and full of themselves. I think they have a chip on their shoulder. They had a bad time inside, and they want to make everyone pay. Yesterday they killed someone over there. A couple of slashes. That's the way it is every day. They rule the roost there, and at night it's terrible. That's why yesterday we were armed when we went there. We had leather jackets with our guns underneath, me and another kid who was working with me. You always have to be on the lookout—those jerks will shoot you in the back and ruin you. One time I went by and Tripa, the guy who's the most trouble, was on the corner, and he greeted me 'Hey, what's up?' as if it was all cool. But I don't trust them: they're treacherous."

A whistle sounds from the group letting the afternoon drift by in the shack opposite. A woman there sells us giant breaded chicken sandwiches and beer from a window. The kids from the slum gather at the door and stare at the three of us against the wall. "It's me he's calling," says Chaías, raising his arm to wave with all the courtesy an acquaintance demands. Just then, Jilguerito, a nine-year-old expertly riding a bike with many gears, comes up to us. He's the son of another hood thief, a distant relative of Frente's. "Tell him, Jilguero, how Frente used to give you stuff," says Orejita, Chaías's buddy. "Tell him that time that you ate yogurt for like a week," he insists. And Jilguerito laughs and says that yes, Frente was good, the best of all, which was why he also threw stones on February 6.

Tripa was one of the Chanos family, a string of brothers selling cocaine, each of whom had set up drug dens within a few hundred yards of each other. In the winter of 2000, the bond of hatred and need between users and dealers tipped over into violence. The Chanos, but above all Tripa, had gained more enemies than clients. Tripa was one of those who, when he was drunk and high, used to shout in the middle of the slum that he was the dealer no one could touch.

Tripa is the kind of character that the thieves of this story call "rats." A rat, but with a lot more power than the Sapitos, kids of the new generation who don't have the protection Tripa could always count on. It's almost a rule: the dealers are hated not only because they are the trap the thieves always fall into through their addictions, but also because most of them can count on operating under police protection. Tripa was a dealer with close ties to the cops, but he was also somebody people hated because he behaved like a cruel, petty tyrant, someone who bragged about the power he had from being untouchable. They'd had enough of the everyday violence of his threats and muggings. Opposite the 25 de Mayo slum, there's a development of apartment blocks where lower-middle-class families live, trying to set themselves apart from their shantytown neighbors. They keep out of it all. They see, but never intervene in, illegal activities. They hope that by being blind and deaf witnesses, they'll be allowed to live in peace, that they'll be free from robberies and extortion. But Tripa was crazy enough to go for them, too. Off his head from drugs, he would steal the plants from their balconies or whatever else they had on them. Just by looking at them and flashing his always-loaded gun, he forced them to give him sneakers, wallets, belts, their bus fare.

Tripa was the antithesis of Frente Vital. It was inevitable that the dealer came to hate the kid who was admired by neighbors for his generosity and respectful attitude. If Frente shared the money he stole by financing a party every weekend, or by buying diapers and medicine for the other gang members' kids, Tripa would be the one who would take away what little they had, protected by his status as a police informer. Tripa was capable of putting a knife to the neck of a thirteen-year-old kid to take his jacket, or snatching a bike from a ten-year-old. Frente Vital was the only criminal to stand up to him, spitting on the ground in front of him and calling him a snitch.

Inevitably, the fight began on a street corner. At first they were just taunts. Tripa couldn't stand Víctor Vital's defiance. He couldn't put up with his comebacks or the way he locked eyes and refused to look away. Worse still was his popularity. He tried to push Frente, until he pushed him too far. "Because he supposedly had more prison cool but never amounted to anything, he wanted to outsmart Victor, he couldn't stand his contempt. I think it was envy, because Frente was Frente, and he was nothing. Víctor would arrive, and everyone would be all over him. Until the day came when Frente said to his face, 'I'm going to take you down,'" recalls Mauro, the old thief who, on the day Frente was shot, wanted to rip the tin roof right off the shack where his friend lay, despite the hordes of police surrounding it. "From then on they started to clash, and the bastard showed that he wasn't afraid." Just as Mauro would do later on to try to save him, in one of these altercations with Tripa, Frente climbed up on top of a shack and challenged his enemy: "Come out, you rat! Piece of shit! Cop! I'm going to kill you!" Twice they had shoot-outs in the slum alleys, and once on the open field, with one at each end, like in a western.

Frente was to die close to that empty lot thirty-six days after his last encounter with Tripa. Frente was walking home along Calle Berutti, coming from Quirno Costa and Pinto. Tripa was on the corner. He said something, nobody remembers what, but they pulled out their guns. Frente fired first. Tripa hid in the first alley of the 25 de Mayo slum, crouching down. Then the Chanos came out shooting to defend Tripa. Frente retreated to the corner of the San Francisco slum. Tripa came out of the alley and ran across the field. On the far side, Frente and Manuel were still shooting, aiming at his head. From out of range, Tripa taunted them. He did a crazy dance, with his relatives covering him. "Shoot, dumbass!" he shouted. It was December 31. The sound of the shots was lost among the festive fireworks.

3

Víctor Vital's sturdy body swayed as he strutted his stuff to the rhythm of the Colombian cumbia he loved. He'd been out on a job and had money in his pockets—he had everything he needed to light up the darkness of the club and the fifteen teenagers dancing together in a circle. Above all, he was looking at Paola: a redhead with a broad smile and big teeth, thin but shapely, and beautiful as she moved, catching his eye. She was Coqui's and Luisito's neighbor from the Santa Rita slums. She'd gone dancing with her girlfriends and through them met Laura and Mariela. Frente waited until the group merged with the sea of moving bodies, then grabbed her hands, pulling her over to dance with him. But all of sudden, there was a push followed by a hard stare, and then—nobody knows exactly how—a fight broke out. Víctor was seized from behind by two security guards, who twisted his arms behind his back, grabbed him by the hair, and threw him out of the nightclub. The others left with him.

The trouble between the two gangs continued at the entrance to Elepé, a club that until recently was on Route 197, near the tracks. Soon after, the police turned up. Paola stayed out of it with the rest of the girls, but she found herself becoming more attracted to Víctor as she watched him standing up for them. "I don't know how many cops beat him up that night, but he challenged them all to a fight. Especially one guy who lives near here—he said he was going to kick his ass. Afterward we all ran because they started firing rubber bullets. And we came here," says Paola, cradling a baby in her arms. Sabina listens, learning details that had been kept from her before. "That morning, the kids came to tell me that Frente had been arrested, and I was really worried, until he turns up with Paola shouting to me, 'Eh, Sotello!' I wanted to kill him. But he was really happy that he had fought and got away." Paola continues: "Of course, they wanted to take him, but I grabbed his hand and pulled him away, and we ran off," she says proudly.

The two of them got together after that. "But it was the sort of relationship where we'd only see each other every once in a while," laughs Paola. He began to go to her place to visit, dressed up neatly and smelling of cologne. She came to see him in San Francisco. "I was seventeen, and he was a bit younger than me, sixteen, I think. . . . I was older. And, well, we had a few parties at my place, with Sabina. I'm not sure why we drifted apart. What can I say? He was a real womanizer. I'd be here one day, and he'd get calls on his phone, then we'd argue about this or that, and drifted apart. . . . But he had a good heart. I always ask people what sign they are, and if they say Leo, I tell them that's the best sign, even though they're such womanizers. Because they know how to treat a woman—they're not all over you, they're really loving and have so much to give. . . . For me, that was a big deal, because he was the only guy I dated who treated me well. What happened to him really got to me, but that's fate. We did think about making Sabina a grandmother, but we were too young . . ."

Laura, Frente's best female friend and one of the few girls in the group who didn't sleep with him, remembers Paola because when Víctor called her "bow legged," she'd come back with "jumbo booty." "He did have a big butt," says María, during the same conversation with Frente's ex-girlfriends. "Sometime later, back there in 25 de Mayo, we started to call him big booty," laughs Laura, leaning on the table at Sabina's where she, María, and Negra, a third girlfriend of Frente's, recall their adventures with the same guy.

"What did he call me . . . what was it again?" Laura tries to remember.

"Droopy booty!" they all shout at once.

"I went by one time, all straight faced: 'Hey, Frente, how're things?' 'All good, droopy booty! And you?' And it stuck. . . . And then he started to call me and Negra 'the twins' because we both had droopy butts."

THE GIRLS LAUGH about Frente as if taking revenge in a small, innocent way. They share stories about their relationships with him without animosity, without the kind of deep jealousies that could arise among the exes of any man who was still living. He got to know most of them when he was in elementary school with his arm in a cast, and they watched him grow up, shooting to fame within the slum and earning the respect of the entire neighborhood. But the girls remember him at the start as a "dumbass," just a kid, somebody who surprised them by turning out to be a winner. "When he started doing well with the girls, we were like, 'Look at this kid, so dumb but he's nailed them all,'" says Laura, and they all laugh. Laura and Valeria were the ones who provided alibis for Víctor with his various women. "He made sure they didn't cross paths, and if they did, he made sure he was looking the other way," says María.

Frente was no good at ending any of his relationships. From the age of thirteen, he hooked up with different girls from the hood and other shantytowns. One who drove him crazy was Belén, until she went off to live in Entre Ríos.[1] "It was right here, in one of the alleys," recalls Valeria, his accomplice. "I remember that on Saturdays we'd get together at her house, and she always wanted pizza . . . so her mom made it for us. Afterward, when it was time to go home, we'd leave and she'd stay up waiting for him. We'd wait for her dad to go to sleep. Her room faced the alley, so we'd hang out with Frente at one end of the alleyway, she'd lean out and signal to us, and I'd help Frente climb in through the window so he could stay there." And Laura says that Belén was the only one who really mattered to him: "Just before he died, he was about to go to Entre Ríos. He had even asked his mother to go with him. He wanted to go to the carnival there to see that girl."

Those short but intense relationships of Víctor's aroused feelings ranging from tenderness to hate among the women in his life when they gathered together to reminisce. One who puts them all in a bad mood is a girl from another hood whom he nearly went to live with when she got pregnant. The sad end to that makes Laura, María, Negra, and even Sabina remember her with contempt. "He was really happy, he said he was going to get a grip, get his shit together. He painted the furniture, got everything ready for the baby. He would say to me, 'Do you want to be its godmother? Because I'm going to do all I can for my kid . . .' Afterward we were all really mad when we learned

---

1 Entre Ríos is a province to the northeast of Buenos Aires.—Trans.

what they'd done. Maybe, if he had . . . I know, you can't blame the past, or start thinking what if this had happened, maybe something else wouldn't have . . . but maybe, if she hadn't got rid of the baby, if he'd been a father, what went down wouldn't have happened. But hey, that's how it goes, that's fate. When it's your turn, it's your turn, I guess."

María is the one who, even after all this time, still seems the most in love with the dead idol. In her, with her long brown body, angular features, short bangs, and silent but defiant stares, lives the conflict of being his girlfriend one day and, a little later, the girlfriend of his friend—in this case, Chaías. Nearly all the women in the slum admit to counting on their fingers to rule out the possibility that María's twins, Víctor Manuel—like Frente—and Joel, were in fact the revered gang leader's, and not Chaías's. But the dates didn't add up. María got pregnant a month after Frente's murder. I met her in Sabina's kitchen, where the TV is always on, during one of the first nights we had dinner together. She came in with the babies—Chaías had asked her to come so that we could meet them.

María is a woman with a short temper and ready fists. When she left the shack she shared with Chaías and his family, she returned to her mother and her stepdad, Chano, the dealer who had always disapproved of her relationship with Frente. María's biological father, though, actually liked Frente and used to spend long evenings chatting with him. María's father is her stepdad's brother. Her mother went on to marry the brother during one of her husband's long spells in prison. Silently, María seems to be doing no more than repeating that old betrayal.

When she speaks, María is a sweet girl, but every now and then when she's telling a story she has an uncontrollable outburst of anger. A few months earlier, Chaías had to stay home for a few days with bruises from his last huge fight with María. He had lied to her, saying he wouldn't go out, but that night there was no shortage of people telling her they'd seen him with someone else. She found them in the bed she and Chaías shared. Enraged, she went after both of them. "We've split up again. That's what we're like, we fight, but we make up. Last night I went dancing and he wasn't there, but I don't care if everything is OK or not. Anyway, even if he's dancing too, I pretend he's not around, I don't even greet him when I go past, it's like I don't even know him. Last night he didn't go out, and now he won't be going out for a couple more months . . . because the other day I beat him up. The thing is, I'm as good as gold, but if you annoy me, then you've got to face the consequences. He betrayed me, and I beat the shit out of him for being such a jerk."

"She stabbed herself in the stomach like eight times the last time I left her," Chaías told me. "And if she gets hold of some girl who's been with me, she wants to beat her up—that's what she's like." Among the girls she had to compete with, the one she really couldn't stomach was Belén, that idealized serious girlfriend of Víctor's who people talk about—the one he was seeing right up to the end. "I already wanted to beat her up, and then one day I was going past her place, around the corner from mine, and she laughed at me from the window. I couldn't hit her because of the metal bars, so I threw a rock and broke the glass. Sometime later, I did hit her. I let her walk out, easy like. She started walking down the street, and then when she wasn't expecting it, I got her. She lowered her guard, and she lost."

María began her thing with Víctor having to be something of a heroine. They met on a Sunday night at Tropitango, and the next day Víctor was arrested. She was sure from the start that he was the one for her, and so she ran away from her stepdad to go to visit him in the maximum-security prison in Mercedes. This was one of a couple dozen times Frente was arrested and put away. 'To top it off, I thought we'd be back earlier. We set out at like eight in the morning, and when we got back it was nearly nine at night . . . and my mom had to keep on making up excuses to her husband, saying I'd gone somewhere nearby, that I'd be back soon, this and that. 'Yes, but she's not here, look at the time.' But I was really happy that I'd seen him, you know, so I couldn't care less what my parents said."

Frente's sense of humor was dark, bulletproof. Nobody remembers him ever being depressed, sad, or down. He never stopped teasing, making fun of people's little flaws or rubbing their mistakes in their faces. He made cracks at his closest friends and his worst enemies. Even the cops weren't off-limits. "At first he was closest to Gastón, Chaías's brother, but afterward, when I went to live with Chaías, those two started to become close. And he was always joking around. He'd say, 'What, has she got you tied down? Can't you come . . . ?' And I was there, and I would just look like this, hand on my chin, watching TV—I wouldn't answer. . . . Everything he said was to get a rise out of you. Or maybe I would call him, just to talk, because I was desperate to speak to him, and he'd pretend he was opening the door and shouting out, 'Hey, Chaías, your woman is calling me!' The worst thing is that I called him all the time. Sabina says I drove her crazy calling and hanging up if she answered instead of him. Sabina got paranoid. She was afraid it might be Frente's father, who turned up every now and then to make a scene, so she got caller ID."

With Paola, too, he couldn't bring himself to call it quits when she found herself a new man. "Sometimes when he'd call, the baby's father would pick up and Frente would say, 'Can I speak with Paola?' And I'd blush and wouldn't know what to do, but I'd take the phone and say, 'Hey, Víctor, how are you?' And he'd say, 'Hey, what's that sonofabitch doing answering the phone?' And the baby's dad would be listening in on the call. And, well, lots of times they did kind of yell at each other, but it never got as far as guns. One time I had come over here, because I had got my hands on a motorcycle. He loved bikes, so I came to find him. We rode all over the place. When I dropped him off, he asked me to go dancing that night. It was a Friday. 'All right, yes.' He was going to come and pick me up at home. But I didn't make it there, because I crashed the bike and my cousin called my boyfriend. 'What did you call him for? Víctor is coming round!' Sergio, my boyfriend, who's known as Bolero, showed up, and a while later so did Víctor, with Manuel. I couldn't believe it! I went out all choked up to see him, and the expression on Sergio's face was unforgettable. . . . And Víctor's like, 'Hey, Pao, what's going on? We're not going to be able to go dancing, are we?' He talked loudly on purpose. He knew Sergio was inside. He said to me, 'What a shame, we won't be able to go to Tropi. Why didn't you let me drive the bike? You wanted to drive and you crashed it.' Then he started to talk about how I'd been on the bike with him. I couldn't believe it. After that Sergio opened the door and left. I stood with them outside, talking. I was scraped all over. My little brother had been with me on the bike, and he was all busted up too. Sergio left the house and went to my grandmother's, out on the highway, and sat there sulking. The others took a cab, and as they went by, Víctor shouted at him: 'Hey, Bolero, you wuss, your girlfriend was riding around with me on her motorcycle. Your girl is mine!'"

Paola still dreams about Frente. She dreams that she's dancing at Tropitango, part of the crowd, thinking that they've had a fight, and suddenly over the speakers she hears "Paola, please head to the exit, Víctor is waiting for you," and she goes out, but there's no one outside. Then, a while later, she goes back to dancing, and again, "Paola, Frente says to hurry up." And she goes out again, afraid he's mad and waiting outside to tell her off for going dancing without him, and he's there with his hands in his pockets and a huge smile: "See how I tricked you? You got scared, right?" In Paola's dream, they go eat a hotdog and then go back to the club, holding hands like a happy couple. "I dream about him a lot. The other night I had a dream, and I told Sabina. And my mom told me that when you dream of someone who's passed away, it's because they want you to go see them, so I told him that for his birthday I'm going to take him flowers. I dreamed I went to see him at the cemetery, and he was standing there and told me he liked yellow roses, that he wanted me to take a yellow rose. I said to him, 'How come you're here . . . if you're . . . ?' And he said, 'I'm always going to be here, I'm always here.' I don't know if it's true, but sometimes I'm at home and there are noises, you hear things, and I think, 'He's here.' Or I think it's my cousin, because my cousin was also killed by the police. But usually I think it could be Víctor, because I dreamed he said he would always be there. Or maybe he'll always be there because I will always dream of him. I think he's a special presence, somebody who might appear, or take care of you. I think he's a higher being because of that superior way he had about him when he was alive. Even though he was a thief, he always had a huge heart. That time with Manuel and Simon when they stole the La Serenísima milk truck and gave the food to the people in the slum, I remember him with a yogurt, sitting on a corner. He was looking at the kids eating the yogurts, and he was eating his and saying, 'This is the life.'"*

* Paola was arrested on the order of a judge from San Isidro. She is accused of killing her mother, who was murdered with a shot to the head as she slept.

4

Before I met Simon, I had been told more than once that he was an expert at holdups and escapes. I also heard that he'd lost seventy pounds in his last spell behind bars. But I was nervous after waiting for a year and a half to meet him, and the passage of time distorted my memory. I had created an idealized image of him that was as stocky and powerful as he appears in the photos his mother and his brothers showed me, or in the self-portrait in oils he painted on the small table of the prison block at Almafuerte. In that, there's a glint in his eye painted with precision on the brown iris; he looks serious and majestic, with the air of a wild, adolescent Elvis Presley. Two years and three months had passed since he'd been put away in a maximum-security facility. On the day I met him, in an empty office, he was standing within a group made up of his brothers, a friend, and his mother. He greeted me warily but squeezed my hand like it was a gun. I had spoken to his friends, among whom he's remembered almost mystically as a sort of hell-raising antihero. The "masters"—that's what the kids who were locked up called any staff member at the juvenile detention center—and other guards described him as a tough leader, uncompromising and intelligent, who said little and had a troubled relationship with authority.

To most of the kids who had been with him in any of the at least twenty-five places where he'd been detained since the age of thirteen, Simon was an example of strength, one of the kids most in the know about how to handle the pain of spending nearly a whole adolescence behind bars. The officers in the institutions where he was jailed told me his fame was such that some visitors asked to see him just to see if everything they'd heard about him was actually true. They were surprised to find him in his cell, concentrating on some book about Che Guevara with the calm gaze of someone who doesn't feel like he owes anyone anything. The image other inmates have of Simon is that of someone able to resist the minimal benefits offered as incentives around the prison, and as capable of challenging authority in order to preserve a modicum of dignity. I saw him raise his eyebrows vehemently when he talked about the street, the violence that breaks out there, the eight bullets in his body, the times when everything became blurred and he thought the last moments of his life were upon him, the instant when he couldn't so much as remember his own name.

In prison there was a point when he started to put on weight, as if the size of his body would make him immune to the police bullets and the shit that went down in the slum. He grew up and hardened in police stations, in juvenile institutions all over the outskirts of Buenos Aires, and along the alleys of San Francisco, 25 de Mayo, Alvear Abajo, Santa Rosa, San Pablo, La Cava, La Esperanza, Treinta, Santa Rita—ghettos of poverty in the north of the capital. In each hood, he had a place where friends would shelter him. At times he exchanged shots with people who dared challenge him, with those who looked at him wrong, or with real enemies. The first time we met, the only thing he managed to tell me about was what happened early one morning—one of those times when suddenly, as if someone had stabbed him with a knitting needle, he felt an odd lightness and warmth in his body and noticed damp blood soaking him. By then, Simon had been arrested so often that he'd become a moving target for the police, especially the ones in San Fernando. "Suddenly, without realizing it, I began to hear 'Simon this, Simon that' and 'The cops have you in their sights, you're a marked man.'" It wasn't even just his nickname—soon, even his full name was well known. His friendships, too: Simon is one of the kids who, during the golden age of street robberies, could squander a small fortune on clubs, dancing, coke, and girls, generously doling out the takings after pulling a job with Víctor Frente Vital, the saint of the young thieves.

Frente had already died from the four nine-millimeter shots that silenced him after his cry of "Don't shoot, we surrender!" when Simon made one of those critical decisions that irrevocably change the path of your life. Simon was having a quiet Friday evening, thinking he might drop a couple of pills as soon as they finished tattooing the dragon on his chest with ink that was decent—much better than what he'd had for the *M* for Mom, the five enormous dots that mean "death to the cops," a cobra, a marijuana leaf, and the name of his dead friend spelled out in capital letters: FRENTE. With the sound of the tattoo gun in the background, his mind searching for something to focus on besides the pain, Simon was planning a trip to Tropitango with Mariela, his girlfriend at the time. After all, his neighbors were scheduled to play cumbia that night. He had known Pablito Lezcano since he was a kid. As soon as we met, he told me that Pablito had taught him to ride a bike way back when, before his singing made him a millionaire and Simon became an underage thief with old-fashioned scruples. Back then, Tropi was the weekend destination; there was always enough money to get a jug of Fernet and Coke[1] with some Rophy thrown in, quenching their thirst until the early hours, when security would round them up like a herd of submissive cattle and throw them out into the cruel light of the deserted streets around the Pan-American Highway near Route 202.

They were just finishing up his tattoo when Adrian "Cabezón" Manso showed up. Strong as an ox, with rock-hard neck and fists, and known for being a skilled and intimidating fighter, he had met Simon in Talar police station, back when that precinct was exclusively for minors. Cabezón, known as Cabe, was put away so often he became one of the kids most demonized and punished by the state's juvenile institutions, and was among those most feared because of that irreversible stigma.

In Simon's own words, Cabe was a kid who was always in trouble. "I met him behind bars, first in a police station, later in juvie. He's younger than me. When I worked with him, he was thirteen and I was sixteen. Now he must be about seventeen. What was he like? The same then as now, just crazy. The kid is crazy, and even worse when he's on pills. Sometimes I'd take him home and ask him to leave his guns behind because it made no sense to carry them all the time, and he'd be like, 'No way, it looks like trouble over there.' Because the guy already had the idea that there's trouble everywhere—he

---

1 Fernet-Branca is a bitter-tasting Italian digestive drink; Fernet and Coke is a distinctively Argentinian cocktail popular with much of the population.—Trans.

already had some longtime enemies, so he was packing wherever he went. He says it's the only way." Simon admits that Manso and he have shared the same fate: spending most of their time in jail. "In that way, we're the same," says Simon. His mother adds: "Back then, he'd be let go on a Monday and be taken back in again the next week. Always."

That's why the day he arrived at the tattoo parlor in the slum and saw Simon sitting there, Cabe immediately told him he was in trouble. "Lend me a couple of guns?" he asked, agitated. "Take three," Simon said, though the slight burning sensation in his chest was growing by the minute. Not even an hour had passed before Manso was back. He was even more desperate. Out there he had a short but impressive list of sometime enemies and—even at just fourteen—a couple of longtime rivals, not to mention the local cops. That day, he came back in a stolen Audi to ask Simon to give him a hand and lend him some more guns. He hadn't slept in two days, and the pills had turned his anxiety into an excruciating, corrosive wound. They went out together, Simon with his fresh dragon tattoo under a black T-shirt. For a moment after they arrived in the slum to pick up the guns, Simon found himself alone in the passenger seat waiting for Cabe. He was looking in the rearview mirror and, every now and then, looking all around to check that the street was quiet. After a few more minutes of waiting, he spotted a kid approaching; at some point he'd had some issue with the guy, though now he couldn't even remember what it was. "This guy is getting closer to the car to stir shit up," which in the slum means a person is acting crazy, pretending to control the street, throwing out insults and threats, and generally putting their life on the line.

The kid had a brick in his hand and was talking. He kept muttering that he needed respect, that he had just gotten back on the streets after being inside.

"Wait a minute, man—take it easy! What's the matter with you? Go home!"

But, Simon says, the kid kept coming, and at that moment, Cabezón Manso came back with the two freshly loaded guns they had dropped by to collect. Simon barely even had time to register the sound of the shots before Cabezón had his foot on the gas and the wheels of the Audi were spinning in the mud of the shantytown's streets, right at the spot where four alleyways begin, spreading like a fan into the interior of the slum. It took less than one clip to take the kid down. Several hours and quite a few pills later, they heard that one of the bullets had gone astray, ricocheting off the thick plaster of the walls and some corrugated iron and killing a little girl who was playing with her dolls in a nearby shack. The girl's family took the boys to court. That homicide brought a whole lot of problems for Simon. When he told me about it in passing, he was casual, just briefly mentioning "a couple of shots." I remembered now how often his mother, Matilde, and Estela, his sister, had told me about the "accident with the little girl." But they never went into detail.

Simon says that following the brief shoot-out, they had no reason to think anyone else had been hurt. That's why he went back to 25 de Mayo after taking the first pills of the night. One of Manso's seven brothers took Simon, riding on his bike's handlebars, to the house of a woman who had protected him since he was just a little kid. On the way, he spoke to Mariela and they agreed to meet up later at Tropi. But when he arrived back home, his godmother Marga had her daughter Bety over, and she noticed that Simon was out of it and had a gun in his belt. She convinced him to lie down for a while, and he fell asleep. When he woke up it was about five in the morning and Mariela and two friends were sitting around the table talking to his godmother. Simon thought they'd still go out to Tropi, but by then it was too late—the others had already come back. Simon was pissed. He hadn't had chance to go out much since he'd been locked up, so missing a long-awaited night out with his girl and his friends upset him to a degree hard for anyone who's never been in jail to understand. "I was mad, really pissed that we weren't going out, that I'd slept the whole Friday night away when I'd been really looking forward to it. Then, around six in the morning, Mariela's cousin comes to warn me that she'd been picked up for the incident with the little girl. They suspected that she was with me when the girl died." This was warning enough to not stick around any of his usual haunts—at his mom's or at one of his brothers' places. He took off, stealing as he went.

"I went to Santa Rita. From Santa Rita I went to La Cava and from La Cava to Santa Rosa. I was there for a couple of days. By this point I was just walking around like nothing was the matter, as if nothing had ever happened," says Simon, lounging on a bench in the courthouse, with his eight-year-old brother lying across his lap. The place was overflowing with juvenile cases, most of them not even concerning actual crimes but about minors who had been left on their own without an adult guardian. Javier, with emerald-green eyes and an angular face, is Simon's older brother. He visits Simon whenever he is on his way from the juvenile institution on the outskirts of La Plata, where he's doing time, to go into court for some reason or other. Like Simon, Javier has known the inside of as many institutions as he has known pretty girls from the 25 de Mayo slum. He's also done the rounds of jail cells in the northern suburbs and has stolen more than he could remember during that half hour one cold morning that we spent together, waiting for Simon in a room full of women anxious to speak to one of the juvenile court's officials.

On the day that Simon was driving around with Cabezón, Javier was with them. Together, they held up a supermarket next to the station at La Lucila, and he remembers they got 860 pesos each. That's why they went to Santa Rosa. At a friend's place, they changed into clean clothes to go dancing in downtown Buenos Aires. They had enough money to buy anything they wanted. Cabezón was keen to get himself off the pills and have a few lines of coke, which could be bought day or night from one of the Toritos—the local coke dealers.

The gang members from 25 de Mayo and San Francisco had known the Toritos of Santa Rosa for a long while. The two groups hadn't exchanged any shots, but that was less to do with the restraint they exercised around each other than with the tension between thieves on the one hand and the dealers and local coke distributors on the other. It's a strange conflict, one that reflects the resentment of the users who put their lives and bodies on the line to get the cash needed to buy drugs when all the profit goes to the dealer and their protectors among the police. That night, a number of those rivalries came into play when Cabezón stood in the doorway and heard the voices inside telling him no, they weren't going to sell them anything. "The Toritos have always been dealers, and no respect is due to dealers. They could make their money stealing, using guns, but instead they stay home selling that shit that ruins people's lives. Everyone is free to do whatever they want, but it's not something I could do, because it would be like going over to the enemy, becoming something else," says Javier, distanced from crime since he left prison and now a scrap collector, a cartonero, like his mother.

That night, when the Toritos didn't want to sell them anything, Cabezón threatened them. Either they sold them the stuff or they'd shoot up their shack. The Toritos had no time to protest before Cabezón and the others emptied their clips into the walls of the shack. The bullets whistled close to the Toritos' sisters, the Toras. "We left their place full of holes," remembers Simon. Afterward, having vented their anger, they went off to sleep. But the Toritos didn't sleep that night. They stayed up snorting their own supply, and by dawn they'd built up enough rage to begin taking their revenge.

One of the owners of the shack where Simon and Cabezón were staying went outside. As soon as he stepped into the alley, one of the Toritos held a gun to his head. Behind him, the rest of the family were pointing their guns at Simon too, looking like a ragtag firing squad. Simon heard the shouts and came outside to negotiate. "What's going on? Keep your cool. You guys are losing it," he said. Simon had a .38 and a .32 at his waist. Behind him, the others readied their guns. The two gangs were only a few paces from each other, so a shoot-out would mean losses for both sides. The Toritos decided to feign a truce and went away.

Simon and Cabezón trusted the ceasefire. They were hungry, so Simon and a friend went out to get some food. As they walked along, one of them ate a yogurt, the other a sandwich. They were headed for a shack where they were going to borrow a gun for a robbery they were planning that afternoon. Without thinking, they strolled past the Toros' alley.

"Hey, you, Manso!" one of them said to Simon, confusing him with Cabezón. And he stuck a gun in his mouth.

"You're Manso the smart guy, aren't you? Do you know who I am? I'm a Tigre fan."

He jiggled the gun slightly.

Gritting his teeth, Simon said:

"What do I care? If you're going to shoot, go ahead and shoot. What are you trying to prove?"

The guy was about to pull the trigger when from the end of the alley, deep inside the slum, somebody else shouted:

"That's not Manso! That's Simon!"

Giving them no time to realize their mistake before they killed the wrong guy, Manso himself appeared on one side of the alley, as if he'd been lying in wait there. He fired with two guns at once. Simon calculated the distance between his hand and the gun pressed against the waistband of his jeans. But they had grabbed him from behind, using him as a human shield, and then threw him to the ground. Simon draws a map of the Santa Rosa slum on a piece of paper, opposite the San Fernando cemetery, near Frente's grave. He draws the corner, the paths, the cemetery, little men running here and there, the trajectory of the bullets, Manso's location, him on the ground, the bullets whistling past his legs. He was hit three times but didn't feel anything. In all of the chaos surrounding Manso, Simon stayed on the ground. Then he reached for his revolver, stood up, and began shooting, looking for a way out. "I ducked into an alley, and they ran off to a house. I kept walking down the alleyway, not realizing I'd been shot. As I was reaching the shack,

I started to keel over, I saw all the blood at my feet. But I wasn't high—it was first thing in the morning, I had just got up. I'd heard the shooting, but until then I didn't know I'd been hit." Halfway up the alley he couldn't walk any farther. "My legs . . . I couldn't feel them. . . . It was as if I didn't have them." Simon has no memory of his rescue. He ended up being sheltered in a shack, lying on a bed, praying to Frente Vital for nobody to find him, for no one to come after him.

"Manso's mother came to get me," Matilde tells me. "I was inside, at Estela's place. She came around asking for me, but nobody would tell her where I was. That's the way it is, nobody wants to give you up. At the corner she broke down and said she wanted to find me because they had killed Simon."

Finally a kid told her where Simon's sister lived, so Manso's mother went to the alley that led to Estela's house in La Esperanza and started clapping her hands trying to get someone's attention. Javier came out to see what she wanted. "They've killed your brother in Santa Rosa," he heard. Without a word, Javier went back to the shack. He went into the bedroom, picked up his guns, and loaded them. Matilde asked him what had happened. "Nothing, Mom, nothing," he said, and he ran off, red in the face. He refused to believe it could be true.

Matilde and Estela came out into the alley. The neighbors told them what had happened. "When we heard they had killed him over in Santa Rosa, we rushed out like we were crazy. I had been doing chores around the house, but I didn't even stop to change my clothes," says Estela. This story of not even being able to change their clothes when they set out to rescue their men or their kids is common among the women of the slums. They figured that this time Simon might really be dead. Still, they got in a cab and set off to rescue him from whatever danger he was in, whether from enemies in other gangs or from the police. They ran to the slum in flip-flops, heading into the first alley they saw, without caring that it was unknown territory, ready to save him by the sheer force of their physical presence, their insults, the shouts they hurled at everyone. They had no idea how to find him or even how to find their way back through the alleys. As they searched the labyrinth with no clue from anyone about where to start, they spotted a trail of blood. They followed it until they came to the shack. "That's where he was, he couldn't stand up."

Simon wasn't complaining about the pain. He could hardly speak. He was more worried about how to escape from the shack and the Toros' fury than about how to look after his wounds and stop the bleeding. He could hear threats coming from outside. They were women's voices:

"The Bersas, go get the Bersas, we're going to blow you away!" the Toras were shouting, telling their friends to get their machine guns.

Suddenly, a police car appeared on the corner. They had come about something else, a less violent incident that had been reported. Matilde had always fought them—the uniformed enemy had always been the only one you would never ask for mercy, the one whose grave you'd vomit on rather than ask them for favors. But feeling cornered, Matilde saw no other way than to leave under the protection of the law. The possibility of death wasn't unfamiliar to her or the others. They took for granted the idea that at some point they might have to confront the dead bodies of Simon, Javi, and Manuel, just as they took for granted that the kids were thieves. They had to help them at times like this, even though they disagreed with their livelihoods. Stealing raised life's stakes. Stealing entailed the possibility of dying in an instant next to a friend in a holdup, or of getting killed at any other moment over the slightest disagreement or act of revenge.

Matilde confronted the police. The Toras were watching from a bit farther away.

"We're taking him in the patrol car!" she said between clenched teeth, as if giving the cops an order.

She tells me she never thought she would ask, "Please, can I get into a police car," laughing out loud at what she now recounts as an adventure. And she went to get her son. They all went in. The place was dark, a narrow cave crowded with junk. Two women were trying to help Simon, giving him water, while outside the Toritos were walking up and down, marking the alley as their turf and saying they could waste anyone for any reason. Matilde tried to lift Simon with Estela's help, but he was too heavy for them. They got hold of his shoulders to drag him along, but when he tried to stand, he couldn't. A boy helped them, and together they raised him like an old wooden plank swollen with damp and rain. He groaned with pain as they loaded him into the police car, pushing him across the back seat. Matilde stroked his head, but between caressing him and reassuring him that he wasn't going to die, she slapped him good and hard to keep him awake and make sure he wouldn't leave her. Meanwhile, at the other end of the alley, Javier was also fighting for his brother, firing a volley of shots to try to rescue him in his own way, unaware that his mother and sister were saving him alone.

For believers, that Santa Rosa incident was confirmation of the myth that the spirit of Víctor Vital could protect his fellow thieves from bullets. Javier entered from the street that borders the left side of the San Fernando cemetery. He was armed with a defective revolver that required him to push the clip after each shot. Manso and another kid from 25 de Mayo followed him armed with two handguns.

They were in a green Ford Falcon. The Toritos and their gang had regrouped on the neighborhood soccer field, apparently not suspecting the others would be back for Simon. They were having a pickup game, keeping one eye on the ball and the other on the street. Javier got out of the car first and walked toward the field. Behind him came Cabezón. When they reached the end of the street, one of the Toros' red Falcons appeared. Javier saw their guns poking out of the windows and shot twice. The players ran from the field to grab their guns—they'd built a full arsenal.

Manso's rear window exploded from the force of a shotgun blast. Javier ran to the cemetery. He managed to run some ten yards between the gravestones, then threw himself behind a headstone. The bullets ricocheted off the marble and nearby headstones. They whistled right past him, but not a single one made contact. "I got off a couple of shots at the Toros, and then they hid. I shot at two or three, and they stayed on the ground." Javier thought there was no escape until he realized he was beside Frente's grave. Seconds turned into an eternity until, suddenly, he saw a bike leaning against the wire fence next to the street entrance. It seemed like it was put there just for him. "I ran, grabbed the bike, and got out of there." He was pedaling desperately, thinking about the miracle for which he would return to thank his dead friend, when he saw police cars with all their lights and sirens on rushing in to stop the shooting. And so, on top of everything else, he had to throw the gun into some bushes in case he was stopped. The next day, with Simon recovering in the hospital from the three bullet wounds in his legs, he went back to retrieve it.

5

This was not the first time Matilde had had to face the future on her own. She had practically been born to that fate: she came into the world in 1957 in Mar del Plata, and her biological father, a rookie in the local police force, died at the hands of a criminal before she was a year old. As a result, Matilde and her older brother left the city to settle in her mother's family village, Chillar, near Azul.[1] At least there her mother was able to get a job doing the ironing at an uncle's dry cleaners, and while she earned a living, the children's grand-parents and aunts and uncles took turns watching them. Matilde remembers her childhood in that small town as a happy time. "They sent me to kinder-garten. I never wanted for anything." When she was seven, her mother met her second husband, and a little while later they all moved to nearby Olav-arría, where he worked in the cement factory owned by millionaire philan-thropist Amalia Lacroze de Fortabat. Matilde and her brother both attended religious high schools in Azul, taken there every day in a horse and cart. But after that, Matilde's life course took her from being a spoiled little girl to be-

---

1 Azul is a town in the province (state) of Buenos Aires, four hundred kilometers from the capital.—Trans.

coming a mother of six children, supporting them through her work gathering cardboard and paper using carts just like those in which she used to ride during her own childhood.

Until she was fifteen, she lived with her mother and stepdad, with whom she got along well. But after a marvelous *quinceañera*,[2] Matilde got the shocking news that a new sibling was on the way. This newcomer turned out to be a girl, which made her arrival even more unwelcome, Matilde admits, though looking back thirty years later, she's critical of her attitude. It got worse: after that came twins. When she was almost sixteen, the shouting and fights between Matilde and her stepfather became unbearable. She did everything she could to leave, not wanting to live another moment with the intolerable competition of his own flesh-and-blood children. The only alternative was to become a nanny for a doctor couple in Olavarría. She worked there for three years, from age sixteen to nineteen. But after that she started to feel frustrated with her employers. She wanted to visit her maternal grandfather back in Chillar, and when they wouldn't let her, she left. She got help from a cousin who was married to a Roma in Mar del Plata. Matilde went to live with her, not knowing that she would ultimately hook up with one of the couples' friends, who was a Roma. She went with the flow. He fell in love with her. Matilde has wonderful photos from that time in which she looks like a pop star, with her straight hair and the greenest eyes on the coast. "The problem is, according to tradition, when a Roma falls in love, marriage has to follow. I didn't like the idea of being stuck forever one little bit, so I left pretty quickly after that." Alone again, she left for Morón on the outskirts of Buenos Aires, going to the home of another family from the Roma community. There she stayed until she found out that not only her Roma boyfriend but also her wannabe father-in-law were coming looking for her. She decided to adopt the plan she had hatched with the friend who was hosting her: both of them would run away from their upcoming obligatory weddings and head to Tigre, where they would take refuge with the girl's relatives.

They arrived at the shantytown of Garrote. They had just finished their dinner when the men of the offended family arrived to bring them back. "They were ready to fight to the death to recover the prize that had slipped through their fingers. We had no way out, it was all or nothing, so I had to jump over the fence at the back of the house." Matilde leapt over the fence

---

2 A *quinceañera* is a big celebration of a girl's fifteenth birthday. — Trans.

as though completing an obstacle course and took refuge on the banks of a tributary of the River Luján. It wasn't deep, but she didn't dare enter the dirty water because she was scared of eels. A man who saw her threw a log as though he were a gentleman from olden times tossing out his cape, and Matilde crossed to the other side.

Her friend didn't manage to escape, though, and she had to go back with the Gypsies. Matilde stayed, living with her relatives. Those years saw the best carnival celebrations in the history of the northern outskirts. The festivities lit up the summer all down Avellaneda Avenue, with dancing throughout Virreyes and the surrounding areas. It was at one of those dances that Matilde met Mario Fuentes, a cheerful guy who played his guitar in backyards and at barbecues. That's how they fell in love: listening and dancing to Los Wawancó, Los Iracundos, Julio Jaramillo, and Rosamel Araya.

They had been together for eight months when Matilde got pregnant with Estela. They piled into his parents' place, and a few years later, Javier was born. He was still only a baby when Fuentes left his job stacking planks at the local sawmill and began seeing another woman. Matilde was never easygoing, so the "other woman" problem brought the couple permanent conflict. Mario began to drink more and more. He was drunk the day they had their last fight, on the day she had finally had enough. When he raised his hand to hit her, she plunged a pair of scissors into his chest, just missing one of his lungs. With the kids still sound asleep in their beds, she left the house, headed for Otero.

Otero is the police station in San Fernando where, in later years, her kids would end up being held on more than one occasion. Matilde had the courage to report Mario's beatings despite being pregnant for the third time, expecting Manuel. She said she was afraid and asked the police to come back to her house with her. They went in a blue pickup, she now remembers. As soon as she walked backed into their place, Fuentes jumped on her like a furious wounded animal. In the short time it had taken her to report him, he had downed a whole jugful of wine. The cops pinned him down and handcuffed him. The noise woke up the kids. Estela, who was just learning to walk, took one of the cops by the hand and led him to the drawer where she knew her father kept a loaded gun.

It took Matilde only a few hours to move what little she had to the house of an evangelical neighbor. With the last of her income as a factory worker, she bought tickets to return to her parents' place in Olavarría. She spent most of her pregnancy surrounded by family, and Manuel was born in the "cement city" at almost the same time as democracy returned to Argentina. Fuentes discovered where they were, and before long he turned up with his mother and a sister-in-law to fetch back his wife and children. He and Matilde got back together, and all of them returned to San Fernando. The honeymoon period lasted until their first fight. She left him again, and during one of those summers, with the Avellaneda carnival in the background, she met Pájaro Miranda. He would become the father of her other two children, Daniel and Gonzalito. "We decided to get married officially, and as payback for what Fuentes had done to me, I registered Manuel as Miranda's son. That was my revenge," confesses Matilde.

That was when I understood why Manuel always told me that he gets on with his real dad and wants to take back his family name; that he has tried to do the official paperwork to change his ID. There was never any love lost between him and Pájaro, but for Mario, his real father, he has nothing but warm feelings: "I still see my old man—everything is cool with him. I go to his place, we get on great. He's a bricklayer's assistant, and he likes cock fighting. He breeds the birds and makes them fight. Others bet, and he gets the money when his bird wins."

When Matilde got together with Miranda, Fuentes wanted his kids back, especially his oldest son, Javier. Matilde decided to get the boy out of the way and sent him to Olavarría. From age three to seven, Javier lived with one of his uncles. Javier has a romanticized recollection of that time in the countryside. "I remember that I had sneakers, I had a school uniform, I went to school, had my milk when I got home, went out to play for a while, did my homework, and by eight-thirty I'd be back inside, no wandering out on the streets."

It was in the mid-1990s that the story of the Fuenteses and Mirandas began to get even more complicated. Until then, they kept the household going thanks to Matilde's work at a factory and Miranda's jobs as a security guard and butcher. Then the factory closed, and Miranda lost both of his jobs, too. A neighbor's imaginative idea offered them a solution: he suggested they buy cheap cleaning cloths and sell them at train stations, from Congreso, in the city center, to Sucre, in the expensive neighborhood of Belgrano. Times were different then, and they managed to sell everything they took into the capital. And since they were returning empty handed, they began to go through all the stuff that the new upper- and middle-class people were throwing away after doing so well in the first period of President Carlos Menem's economic reform. That was a time when the better-off bought new furniture, appliances, and electronics. Matilde and Miranda would go through the garbage. "We became garbage collectors, at first almost as a hobby, to take advantage of what was there, and afterward to make a living from it." Matilde and her children were among the first in the San Francisco slum to use a horse and cart to collect valuable garbage. That was when Sarratea wasn't yet a street and the shacks were spread around a field that now sits opposite a warehouse. These days, Matilde's two-room shack stands facing what remains of the slum after the area was developed. At the back there was a stable that later became the secret entrance for the young thieves trying to escape police bullets.

Matilde and her children were among the first people to find themselves out of work and relying on belongings pulled from other people's garbage after President Menem's policies took hold. At that time, the devastation of the middle class, even the lower middle class, seemed impossible because of the impregnable strength of the one-to-one exchange rate with the U.S. dollar. At first, Matilde says, this scrap collection work brought in enough to feed the family, although she could never give her kids treats like the ones they saw the better-off children in Belgrano getting. Javier, Manuel, and Simon had never really settled in at school, and they soon left altogether. Their personalities were by now already well defined. Always the quietest, Manuel stayed to one side and allowed Javier, the oldest, to take the leading role. After his return from Olavarría, Javier gradually became the troublemaker at school. The two brothers looked more alike back then than they do today, and when it came to identifying the culprit of their mischief making at school, the teachers would get them mixed up. It was common, Matilde recalls, for the boys to be sent to the principal together and for them to come home with ears red from being pulled. The school authorities tried to make them confess which was the troublemaker, as though they were identical twins, but they never succeeded in getting the brothers to betray one another. Nevertheless, they would come up against the same kind of punishment time and again throughout their adolescence, when the juvenile courts locked them up for long stretches. But that was a few years later when, almost without warning, Javier, Manuel, and Simon turned to armed robbery as a means of getting enough money to live their own version of the high life that the rich enjoyed during a time of large-scale government corruption, trafficking, and theft.

A WEEK AFTER I had met Simon, we had an appointment to see each other again and talk more. Early in the morning on the day before our meeting, I woke to the sound of the telephone ringing. I let the machine answer. Still half-asleep, I heard Sabina Sotello's voice: "Sabina here, leaving you a message. . . . Unfortunately, Matilde's son has had an accident. He's in a coma in intensive care. And they're trying to get Simon out of jail to see his brother, so Simon's not going to be in a great state of mind. Call me later. Bye."

I thought it must be Manuel, who had been at large since March. I was afraid he had been wounded in a shoot-out and that he might not have kept his promise to give up crime. I soon learned what had happened: Daniel, Matilde's fourth child, age fourteen, was returning home on the "white train," the one provided for cartoneros to come back from the capital with everything they have collected, when he put his head out of the open window to check what train station they were coming up on. It took just a second: his head smashed against a metal pole. He was with Javier, who luckily managed to hold him and keep him from falling onto the tracks and under the wheels of the train. Like always, the train car was full. The passengers who saw the accident or heard it were hysterical because the train didn't stop: they were passing by San Isidro station, but that's not one of the white train stops. The driver ignored the screams ("Stop, you sonofabitch, stop for God's sake!") and the pounding on the floor of the train car. The train carried on as usual, and Javier had to wait until they went past Beccar and reached San Fernando before he could call an ambulance. "We laid him on the ground. You can still see the blood stain on the platform," he says. The ambulance took twenty minutes to arrive. The only one of Matilde's sons who had not turned to crime was dying because of a blow caused by the same systems of social exclusion that had given rise to all the bullets his brothers had managed to avoid.

THE NEXT DAY I set out early for San Fernando. Simon was due to appear in court and knew his family would ask permission for him to visit Daniel in the hospital. It was a long wait at court, with Matilde and her son doing all the paperwork in different offices on different floors of the building. Simon had been out since the previous night because he got word as soon as his brother was taken into neurosurgery, and he had refused to return to the prison. His mother had been asked to sign a form accepting responsibility for any escape attempt. "I'm not dumb enough to try to escape with my brother in this condition. It's only because we want to be together as a family. If I wanted to, I would have escaped already, sir," he told the court official he had to report to. His mother also spoke on his behalf: "He has the right to be with us in this situation. His brother was on the white train . . ." She couldn't go on: having to recall the accident reduced her to tears again. The court official she was speaking to had known her for six years through the escapades of her three sons; he told her there was no need to go into the details. "No need to explain—you're free to go."

While his mother was making her way from office to office, Simon told me about his last robbery, which never even got off the ground. It had been planned for a Friday in June 1999 on the outskirts of the 25 de Mayo slum. He was with another kid, one of the older thieves, a guy only he, Frente, and Manuel, among all the kids of the hood, were allowed to go out stealing with. It was seven in the evening, and they were like caged rats, prowling around and jumping up and down in their cushioned sneakers, running from one shack to another, keeping an eye out for the cops who could take them in just for carrying firearms. Because there was a delay in setting off, Simon admits, they did "have a go at a couple of guys from Aviación," a shantytown on 202nd Street and the Pan-American Highway near Don Torcuato. With the few pesos they stole, they went to the local store. As they were passing a friend's shack, she called out, "When are you coming round for a drink of *maté*?" "I'll be right back," Simon told her.

He walked toward the highway, but he had hardly turned the corner when he heard *bang!, bang!, bang!* echoing nearby. His reflex was to shoot off a few rounds into the darkness before he managed to gather all his strength and leap toward a neighbor's shack in search of refuge. As soon as he hit the ground, he could feel warm blood in his gut and arm. He could hear people running toward the shack, but he knew he had no way to defend himself. His vision began to blur, and he lost track of his surroundings in the shack. He couldn't see the woman who lived there; he was just shouting out for them not to kill him.

"Get out of here, or we'll shoot you too!" one of the San Isidro cops told the woman.

Until he felt the cuffs squeezing his wrists, Simon didn't know it was cops who were after him. "I couldn't see anything—everything was blurry, and I was choking on blood. To top it off, when they had me on the floor, one of them put a gun to the back of my head and pulled the trigger." By some miracle, it didn't fire, so instead they used that same gun to beat his head.

"I knew he'd go for it!" said one cop, gloating because Simon had reacted as soon as he heard shots, giving them the excuse they needed to return fire and attack.

"I knew he'd go for it!" said another.

They were clearly happy to cart him off. But they didn't put him into an ambulance: they just put him in their pickup. Still more punishment was meted out on the journey. It's a familiar routine: the police take turns delivering the blows as if they are sharing loot, as if each blow, whack, and kick is part of some symbolic prize they are dividing up among themselves. "They started to beat me up. They would take turns. Suddenly they would stop, and the one driving would come into the back to hit me. When he got tired, another one would replace him, as each of them took his turn." Then they got close to the train tracks and one of them shouted:

"Now we're going to finish you off!"

Simon thought this was the end, that either through beating him to death or shooting him in the middle of nowhere, they were going to do away with him once and for all. Until he heard:

"Nah, leave this shit to die in the hospital! He's not going to make it!"

When they got to the hospital, they left him on the floor of the emergency room, where he lay until the medics put him on a stretcher. "After that I don't remember anything. The only thing I remember is a guy who came over, a nurse, who said to me, 'Man, take it easy. God loves you,' and patted my back."

When Simon finished talking about that almost fatal night, and because the nurse's reassurance made me think of Frente and the saving powers many believe he has, I asked him if he had thought about his friend, who has now become a kind of saint. "I was lying there, and to tell you the truth, I was in a bad way. I thought I was dead. They put two bullets in me," he said, showing me the mark of the shot on his arm, and then raising his checked shirt to show me the scar he has two inches below his sternum, which looked more like a misshapen belly button than like the trace of a brush with death.

"How many times have you actually been shot?" his mother asked.

"Eight," he answered.

"Do you have any bullets left in your body?" I wanted to know.

"Well, he has one in his liver . . . ," replied Matilde.

THAT DAY, WITH Daniel in intensive care, Matilde and Simon, Estela, Javier, Manuel, and a good part of the slum had had no sleep. When I saw them at the courthouse, Matilde's eyes were red and Simon's skin was ashen. Daniel had been operated on overnight, and his family had been waiting three hours for news. Matilde had had to sign a document before the operation in case things went wrong: "The paper said that he might be disabled, or a vegetable, or blind, or he might simply die." Matilde says she didn't want to sign, that she felt confused; she couldn't work out whether it was right to accept responsibility, but she could see no alternative. She stared with her beautiful green eyes into the beautiful green eyes of her oldest son, and then Javier lowered his gaze to indicate yes. Back in the slum, the prayers multiplied. Some took off to Frente Vital's tomb with offerings for Daniel, the same types of offerings usually given when asking for police bullets to miss their mark; others lit candles in their homes. Many brought just themselves, the only thing they possessed, to stand alongside the family in the uncomfortable waiting room.

A makeshift camp gradually built up on the first floor of the hospital: over the next few days there were never fewer than four people waiting for the bad news. And during visiting hours, there were up to twenty at a time. Daniel's siblings and mother lost count of how many came to be with them. Among them that afternoon I met three women who had played a central role in Simon's life: "Grandma" Marga and her daughters Emilia and Graciela. Marga wasn't really Simon's grandmother, but that was how she was known in the slums, and Simon had lived in her house during the last few months while he'd been at large. Emilia was Simon's godmother and the first wife of Mauro, the thief with the old-style honor code who mentored Frente Vital. Graciela was the mother of Facundo, who had been the fourth member of the gang back when they were an inseparable group, whether headed to the clubs, committing a robbery, or just supporting one another. That was when I learned that Marga was also the *mai umbanda* (religious leader) of the slum. When we were introduced, she invited me to visit her.

Among the paperwork that Matilde had filled out at the court while getting the judge to let Simon out for a few days was a form asking the local government to cover the costs of Daniel's hospitalization. She had only just managed to collect enough money for the supplies he needed. It was the end of the month, and I was broke, too, unable to help. The same was true for most of those who had come to see what they could do. The only things there were plenty of in the waiting room were cigarettes. There was no food; because of the anguish, anxiety, and nerves, nobody had felt hungry. We were all waiting for five in the afternoon, the only time you could visit patients in intensive care. I didn't know whether I should go in, but when Estela and Matilde showed me where to stand in the line, it became clear that I was expected to. Relatives of all the patients were crowded along a corridor in intensive care: contorted faces, murmurs about the latest bulletins, the hospital silence broken by the respectful sounds of grief. One by one, we filed in.

Matilde came out after ten minutes. Then it was the turn of Daniel's siblings. Simon was in for just a few minutes. Later he confessed to me that he couldn't face it; he didn't know what to do beside the high bed, with Daniel's shrunken body connected to all kinds of tubes, drip feeds, and machines, his head swollen like an overripe fruit. I felt the same. We were told we could speak to him, that maybe he could hear us. It was impossible to recognize the face of the boy he had been. I managed to say that he was loved, that outside there were more people than he could ever have imagined would visit a patient.

In the waiting room, the neighbors and relatives were asking Simon how his brother was. "It's up to him," he told them all. And with every new arrival, the scene was repeated: the newcomer greeted Matilde, Estela, Manuel, and Javier, and then stayed quietly in a corner until someone said, "That's Simon," and they realized this was the boy who was imprisoned in Almafuerte, now so changed after two years and three months inside. Simon enjoyed the shock he caused. And no sooner had he greeted them, he would come out with ironic comments about their appearance: "You look like shit, man," or "You're so fat, Mary!" or "You're looking old!" Unintentionally, Daniel's tragedy was bringing Simon back into shantytown life, and from that hospital waiting room he began to see the changes that had taken place while he was inside. We spent another hour there, until Simon wanted to go back to the house for a shower before he returned to the permanent vigil at the hospital.

We arrived at the slum in a cab and didn't go to his mother's house, but straight to his grandmother's. Matilde and Estela would come by later: they had to see the mai to ask her to intervene to help Daniel stay alive.

I didn't realize that this was the first time Simon was setting foot back in the home he'd had to leave when he was locked up. Emilia and Graciela were sitting around the kitchen table, with the Moira Casán show on the TV. On the screen, a dark-haired woman and her teenage niece were fighting, the first accusing the other of stealing her husband from under her nose. "My baby looks all grown up," Marga said, stroking Simon's chin. The women seemed happy to have him back. They began to reminisce about the time when Simon was on the streets and brightening their days. "You know that Facundo is inside now. Well, when they all started to get put away, and my nephew, too, we'd all hold on to Simon, who was still on the loose," said Emilia, the hairdresser with cropped bright-blonde hair. She had been Mauro's wife when they were teenagers, and she later got together with another career thief who was still in Olmos prison for a big heist. "You know how it is. Waiting so long for him to get out, and in the end he was only around for a couple of weeks before he was sent back in again." Graciela, thinner than her mother and sister, recalled: "By the time I knew Simon, he was already a handful. Facundo was about fifteen, and he was a bit younger. The first time they were arrested for stealing a bike, it was based on a false accusation by an old woman from around here. When we went to the police station with Matilde and I saw him in cuffs, I was heartbroken because I didn't know what to do. Afterward you learn how it is and get more used to it."

On that occasion, Graciela went to rescue them from the local police station with Matilde, who by then was an expert in how to talk to the police when one of her boys was arrested. "Bring me the woman who's accusing him!" Matilde shouted at an officer. Graciela says she was surprised how well Matilde could argue and defend her son from the police. She learned a lot just watching her. After that incident with the bike they hadn't stolen, the boys kept getting arrested every week or so. "They always got arrested together. Sometimes they even turned themselves in when one had gotten away, so they could be together." Simon laughs and says that yeah, once he asked the cops at Pacheco to arrest him. "'Hey, officer, I was stealing with them, take me in,' I said to the guy. And he was like, 'What the heck? Get out of here, kid, you're not part of this.' And I said, 'But you know, I was there, and if not, I can steal something now so you can take me in. Go on.' I was such a pain that in the end he said, 'OK, if you really want to be locked up, c'mon.'"

I was going to interview their grandmother next. She was going around the kitchen preparing something in a square bottle that was full of stuff: amulets and chains, tiny clay figures, little bells. She was waiting for a woman who had an appointment with the mai but hadn't turned up. "If you're not in a hurry, you can wait for me, because I need to do a little job first," she said, and disappeared down an alley wearing a white T-shirt and long, flowing skirt. "The 'African lady' is coming," said Graciela and Emilia a few times while they passed around the maté. I thought that must be somebody's nickname. Simon asked for a piece of paper and a pen. He sat down to write to Facundo. While the women and I carried on talking about times gone by and the Moira Casán show, two little girls were playing between the yard and the kitchen, laughing at something I didn't quite catch. The grandmother was busy in the next room. I had no idea what she was doing, although I suspected it was an Umbanda ceremony.

I began to hear phrases of *portuñol* (a mix of Spanish and Portuguese) spoken in a gruff voice I hadn't heard from the grandmother before. When

I turned in my chair, I discovered that the only thing separating the kitchen from the other room was a white curtain. Through the slightly translucent material I could see the silhouette of Marga in her long, bulky mai skirt. She had also put on a threadbare broad-brimmed straw hat that she had decorated with flowers, scarves, and talismans. She was readjusting it with both hands every now and then, and was swaying in front of an altar covered with plaster saints and flickering candles. "*Procure o minimo*," she said suddenly. "You don't know what a woman's love is like," she spat. Outside, the afternoon light was gradually fading. Through the kitchen door I could see the yard, with some rusty chairs around an old garden table, and beyond that the line of the horizon over an empty lot. As the sun went down, the sparse lights of the shanty came on. Simon finished his letter, lengthy paragraphs written in a neat hand, and Chaías arrived to ask the mai for a cure. They invited him into the temple, and then me too. The mai spoke Brazilian Portuguese like a tourist who's just landed in Florianópolis, but with the spirit of a child playing with dolls, changing her words to make them fit each different character: a bad, chastising mother; a sweet, good grandmother. The mai was the same grandmother from just moments ago, but now she was possessed by the spirit of the "African lady," a mischievous old woman.

Access to the room was not via the curtain, but through a door in the side passage. As soon as you went in, the mai was there, standing next to Graciela, who quietly translated the questions and answers and explained, for a novice like me, how it all worked. "The mai says you can ask about something, any problem." I didn't know what to say. "The mai says that there could be bad people you have hurt who now want to hurt you." Then the African lady said she could do something about the supposed revenge if she were given seven colored stones and a long list of offerings. "Mai says that afterward my mother, Simon's grandmother—the owner of the body possessed by the African lady—will tell you exactly what you need so that she can give you some protection." Mai's interest then turned back to Simon, her favorite. Simon wanted support from the women to encourage him to seek out Mariela, who had been his girlfriend until his long stay in Almafuerte. After such a long wait, Mariela had moved on and was living with another man. That afternoon at the hospital, other guys from the 25 de Mayo slum had talked about a supposed shoot-out between these two rivals competing for Mariela's heart. It struck me as almost endearing, this gossip about a love story where no one seemed to want to take sides, especially since it was clear from the calm expression on Simon's face that even he was hardly feeling aggressive: he seemed almost like a baby in a man's body. The mai was adamant about this, though. As a grandmother—before taking on the spirit, without the Brazilian hat on her head—she had already told Simon, "You can't do it!" And he, grasping at the cloth of his loose shirt, had lowered his head contritely and said, "I still have to bind up my heart with tape."

But the grandmother would not budge, and concluded in words he could not fail to understand: "It's over."

When she became the mai and he again asked her advice, she once again dashed his hopes: "That woman is a whore! She messes with you and then goes off with other guys. She sleeps with other men. She's no good for your heart. She can only bring you trouble." (*Mulher fica como una putana. Mulher vai fifar con você y despois fifa con otro meninos. Despois fica con outro homi. Mulher no sirve para corazao de você. Ela pogi traer problema para você.*)

She said this in the rasping voice that witches are imagined to have, something like the healer who appears in *Nazareno and the Wolf,* but all in that unique mixture of Spanish and Portuguese that is so tricky to follow.

"But I just want to be with her for one night, mai. After that I don't care."

"If you don't care, then go ahead! Go, go, go! You're so stubborn!" said the mai, raising her hand in the air in a gesture that could mean *go to hell,* or *do whatever you like,* or *I give up.*

After that they brought Matilde in. She kissed the mai's hand and told her about the boy fighting for his life. The mai went over to the altar, said a prayer, lit another candle, and rummaged through her things. From her shelves, she took more large candles, necklaces, and amulets. There was a bottle of perfume on a small table. When an eighth person arrived—up to that point it was Simon, me, the two little girls who were still laughing quietly, Graciela, Chaías, and Matilde—the mai got us to sit on the chairs around the room decorated Umbanda style.

The mai had hung on her walls all the folk objects that she had found or that had been given to her during her long tenure as healer and medium. On one side, there were drums from northern Argentina; on the other, Mexican hats, and farther away, masks from a southern tribe. All of a sudden, she lit a cigar—a real cigar—to which, as a touch of sophistication, she added a holder. When all of us were seated, she started to perform on the floor. Like a young girl, she took the skirt she had made from material with a very pale geometric design and folded it between her crossed legs. She shook the bottle like a maraca, and after every couple of drags on the cigar, she took a swig of alcohol.

She told Matilde to get hold of a chicken—red or yellow but definitely not black. "As it happens, a woman who lives near you has some that should work," she told her. Matilde whispered in my ear, "There *is* an old lady on my block who has loads of chickens." "Don't worry—if it's stolen, all the better," said the mai—this seemed to be a central theme of the information I was to receive from the African lady.

Graciela attempted to explain. "The mai thinks that stealing isn't always a bad thing. Because when she was an African woman five thousand years ago, her people ate anything—roots, fruits—and some of them wanted to hoard food, so they stole it from them. That's why it's not always bad to steal."

Graciela is a soft-spoken woman who was making an effort to keep the conversation going between us, the believers, and the mai, who every once in a while appeared to lose control. Suddenly, she took a long swig of alcohol, drew deeply on her cigar, and peered at me from under the brim of her hat:

"You have a problem."

Starting from that affirmation, the mai diagnosed that I had evil enemies whom I had harmed, and on top of that I was exhausted, weighed down by listening to so many stories of death. Following this pronouncement, she proceeded to cleanse Simon and Matilde before turning to do the same to me. She stood me barefoot in the middle of the small altar and began to rub me down with a succession of ten different-colored candles, rolling each one over my clothes before starting with the next. She was breathing heavily and at one point turned around to see who else was looking on.

"*Muito forchi*, very burdened," she said.

She took the perfume bottle, poured some on her hands, then wiped my face, neck, and hands with it. The scent of the cheap perfume overwhelmed me, and when I stepped back and put my shoes on, Simon and Matilde looked at me and said I looked different, changed. They both agreed that they felt much better, relieved of the tiredness of not sleeping for two days while they waited for news of Daniel.

WE SAID GOOD-BYE, and the mai continued with her ceremony. We crossed the division between the 25 de Mayo slum and La Esperanza. On the corner by Frente Vital's house, we stopped to greet the kids hanging out there, including the ironically nicknamed "Legs," an older kid born without legs who was sporting a shiny new wheelchair. He greeted us politely and—out of respect for Matilde—allowed the joint he was holding to burn down, half-hidden by the crook of his fingers. Respect in the slums is like that: it doesn't matter that Matilde has seen hundreds of joints being smoked, or that it's obvious she would never chastise anybody for it—she's still Simon's mother and a lady. "How's the boy, ma'am?" Legs asked her. "Still the same," she replied, and told them about the train company lawyers who had come to visit her in the hospital waiting room, and others who appeared later offering their specialized services in accident and compensation cases. "If the guys from the company come and offer two thousand dollars, or even ten thousand, you have to turn them down, because they'll have to pay out way more," two women said to her, leaving her a full-color flyer advertising their work. "I didn't smack them because we were in a hospital, but I told them that if they thought that being a cartonera meant being illiterate or ignorant, they were very much mistaken. Because I know very well what my son's life is worth, and if we go to court, it will be so that there's justice for everyone, so that it can't happen again."

Matilde wasn't blinded by her son's tragedy. As though she had been learning for years what to do if this happened, from the day of the accident she maintained that its true cause was that the white train was deliberately made for those stripped of their rights. Even though they all pay for their tickets, the car they travel in is taken from a disused train emptied of seats. This way the "undesirables" and their carts don't bother the other customers. With no glass in the windows and no lights, the cars of the white train operate outside of any regulations; as the conductors are the first to admit, these cars should not be on the tracks at all. The one Daniel was on didn't stop despite all the shouts coming from the cartoneros because it didn't even have an emergency brake. And Daniel hit a metal fence that was put up around the station so that nobody can slip onto the platform without paying.

We walked on toward Estela's house. On the corner of her street there were more kids, so we stopped there with Simon. The din of badly played drums filled the block. It was a rehearsal, but the kids didn't know for which band. I thought it might be the Jedientos del Rock—Estela and Manuel's neighbors—or Pablito Lezcano, the millionaire who remained in the slum despite his wealth and even built a recording studio in his childhood home. But when Simon asked, the kids said that it was just some jerk. There were seven of them leaning against the wall and a girl sitting on the stoop writing out the words of what looked like songs or poems on a blank sheet of paper. Among them was Chicote, a friend of the family who came to the hospital every day. He was younger than the rest, a sixteen-year-old who divided his time between armed robbery and boxing, occasionally competing as a featherweight. "I waited for you, and you weren't there," he rebuked me: we had agreed earlier to meet in the hospital so that I could interview him, but the ceremony with the mai had intrigued me so much that I'd lost track of time and forgotten about him. "Come on, say hi, don't you say hello anymore?" the dark-haired girl who was writing said accusingly. Chicote didn't reply, just laughed, looked at her, and went quiet. A minute passed with no one saying much of anything. Simon was the only one talking: "Look at this one—he's gotten so big! With an earring, too," he teased one of the kids who had grown up while he was doing time. "And this one, he's gotten so fat!" A long-haired guy came up and greeted each kid by name, making a face like *Who're you?* when he stretched out his hand to Simon. Simon enjoyed the anonymity. "That guy's like, 'Who's this new one on the block?'" he laughed when the kid was gone.

I left them to go ahead half a block to the entrance to Estela's alley, where she and Matilde were chatting with some friends. Elsa, a neighbor whom Simon greets as "auntie," was standing in her doorway. We were there for half an hour discussing Daniel's condition. Simon went into Elsa's house to greet Elsa's husband, who was bedridden. Elsa came out with a plate of breaded chicken she had made, then went back into the house and returned with four fresh eggs. The little shop that gave Estela credit was closed, so though nobody had said anything, it was clear that Elsa's gift was all they were going to have to put on the table that night. Matilde disappeared without a word: despite already having gone forty-eight hours without sleep, she went off to get the yellow chicken that the mai had suggested she steal.

Estela's house is the last one down an alley that seems like one long entrance to a single house. Along the path, there are dozens of shacks from which you can smell the scent of stews brewing and hear the sound of TVs blasting cumbia at full volume, laughter at the usual jokes mixed with insults and the occasional silence. Estela has two rooms with peeling walls. In the kitchen there was a TV showing *Pop Stars*, the program chosen by her kids, who range from two years old to seven. Simon took the remote, sat down, and switched to the film channel, which was showing an American movie about a gang of thieves who end up killing each other as the plot moves along. "In prison, I spend the whole time watching movies, nonstop," he told me. After that he began to talk about soccer and how much he enjoys sports shows where the commentators spend the whole time arguing about every little thing.

The first thing Estela did was to start heating the water so Simon could bathe. She heated the water in the boiler, gave him a towel, and told him he could get undressed in the other room. Simon preferred to go into the bathroom without undressing, and a few minutes later shouted out that the towel had fallen on the piss-wet floor. Estela brought him another one. She gave him a new pair of cargo pants to change into, and Simon tried on a couple of hoodies until he found one he liked. He was pale, paler than in the morning. His skin had become so translucent that the veins at his temples stood out like blue threads. Prison, and above all the dark cells in police stations and the maximum-security wings of institutions, turns the prisoners' faces nearly see-through; when they come out, that's the most obvious sign that they've been inside. Though that's not why people seeing Simon after such a long time don't recognize him, or look at him as if they've just seen a ghost walking the dim streets of the shantytown—it's more that, though time seems to stop when you're locked up, when you get back you have to face the unavoidable reality that time has actually been moving all along. That's the real cause of the exile that results from having been imprisoned.

Estela fried the breaded chicken and heated up stale bread to make sandwiches for everyone—her four children and the three of us. Simon and I got bigger servings than the kids, with a fried egg on top. Even though we met midmorning, this was the first time we had eaten all day. By now we were all hungry, a hunger I had learned to control, knowing that there was nothing to eat. We ate our sandwich with a slow pace that belied our appetites. "Is it good?" Estela asked. And she laughed as we mumbled that it was. "Well, you'd better not want more, because there isn't any." Despite saying this, she surprised us with two last small sandwiches as a treat. Then the meal was truly over, and the two of us set off for the hospital again. But first, Simon wanted to call in on Cachi, one of the slum's more established dealers. "I'm going to ask him for some dough, and we'll see if he gives us a couple of lines. He's a good guy, always up for it," he said.

Cachi's place was less than two blocks away, and we didn't run into anyone on the way. The streets of the hood, the lengthy alleys, looked like a deserted stage set for a scene of poverty. "This place is dead," Simon said to me. At the dealer's house, his wife came to the door. She recognized Simon but didn't make any comment about his being back. "You want to talk to Adrian?" she asked. We waited a couple of minutes outside until a man with a face worn from thirty-five misspent years came out. "How you doing, Simon! How's it going?" "All right," said Simon, and started the kind of circuitous conversation full of set phrases that you might expect of two people seeing each other again after a long time and finding that they actually have nothing left to talk about. Soon enough, Simon got to the point and asked him for money for a cab to the hospital. "Yeah, sure," said the dealer, and he went in to get it. He came back and gave him ten pesos. Then, leaning back against the wall, he gave a brutal assessment of the state of things in the slum: "Everything's dead here. Not even the thieves are left," he said. "Maybe there's a bit of movement now, but very little. You've no idea what this place was like in January and February. Nobody had a dime. I have no idea how we pulled through." "But there's money on the streets," Simon said, holding on to the fantasy of going back to breaking into houses where the rich keep their money in the closet. "No, that's over. Now, to top it off, the cops are worse than ever. They do what they want, they kill you like a dog. The truth is they rule, that's the truth."

The description of the mess that had become of the shantytown where, when Simon had left, the guys were still playing cumbia night and day was so dire that he didn't even bother to ask the dealer for some coke to combat his exhaustion. We crossed the street toward a taxi stand by the nearby apartment blocks. It was no use: there was no way we could convince the old guy with a face like a dog to call us a cab. He didn't care about my ID or press pass. "Even if I ask them, no driver will take you," he explained calmly, standing next to a dark-haired woman who was fuming because she couldn't find a taxi that would pick her up from near the slum either. We had to go to find another taxi stand, where they finally agreed to give us a ride after the guy recognized Simon as the same kid who, years earlier, used to visit his house. "Don't you remember me? I've been to your place—my brother went out with your sister," Simon reminded him. The guy smiled when he worked out who Simon was, and he stopped writing down my ID number on the list where unknown clients are recorded.

Even so, the driver of the cab we eventually got into was terrified. Before leaving the slum, we went by the mai's house—we'd agreed that I should interview her, so I got out there and said my good-byes. The mai had become Grandma Marga once more, but before hugging me hello she gave me a piece of paper on which she had written down everything I needed for the cleansing ceremony that would protect me from my many supposed enemies. "Ten red and white candles. Seven candles of any other color. Five yards of green, red, and yellow ribbon. An empty tin of sweet potato jam. Seven different-colored stones. Seven white carnations and seven red carnations. One brick (stolen)."

6

Brian was beating his chest and jumping up and down, as if alerting his armed-to-the-teeth neighbors to their target. Age sixteen, Brian had short blond hair and the torso of a twelve-year-old. At that moment, his face was twitching as if he were possessed—the result of three straight days of pills and alcohol—and he was bounding and waving his arms like a player on a basketball court responding to the cheers of hundreds of fans. But in the bright sunlight of that Saturday afternoon, Brian was actually leaping about on the hot asphalt of General Pinto Street wearing nothing but his soccer shorts, beating his chest with his left hand while he spun his gun on the index finger of his right. Spread across the street in front of him was a growing lynch mob hurling insults his way. From across the neighborhood, men of all ages had gone to retrieve their guns hidden in closets and the depths of drawers, keen to blow him away. They had put up with his holding up Doña Rosario, the oldest grandma on the block; with his putting his gun to a little girl's head just to steal her bike; with his mugging Frente Vital's mother, of all people; and—to top it off—with his trying to shoot Rana over a minor disagreement. Rana had beaten up one of the Sapitos, Brian's only friends in the world and members of a precarious gang of "rats," as they call them in the slum—"those who steal from their neighbors and eat without caring who they rob for food and drugs."

MONTHS BEFORE, I had arrived at the shantytown around midday with photographer Alfredo Srur to find Rodolfo, one of Sabina's neighbors, sitting on his doorstep, carefully repairing an old truck engine. The slum was sparkling in the sun despite the misery, and the smell of frying food wafted out a nearby window. A group of kids was playing at the intersection of French and Pinto, while others were kicking a ball around in the empty lot where the huge neighborhood fight against the cops had gone down in the pouring rain on the night Frente was killed. Pato, Víctor's brother, had the day off from the supermarket and was making the most of it, setting up a grill on the sidewalk and cooking two chickens for lunch. He was in a great mood that day, flirting with a dark-haired girl in tight jeans who was coming and going from the alley next to his house. When she reappeared with a thick steak in her hand, Pato obligingly offered to add to the grill.

After having lunch with Alfredo, Chaías, Pato, and Tincho—one of my guides during my first visits to the slum—we went to visit Víctor's grave in the San Fernando cemetery. Pato took the banner he'd had made for his brother, which featured a caricature of Frente smiling. He also took T-shirts depicting Frente trampling a cop's head, the cop's eyes popping and his tongue hanging out as he's crushed under the young thief's sneaker. Sporting the new shirts, the boys made their usual offerings.

In addition to the municipal caretakers who spend their days in a gloomy office next to the entrance hiding from the sweltering heat, the cemetery is also patrolled by plainclothes cops. When I first visited Frente's shrine, his mother told me that as soon as the kids started hanging out around his grave, adding the aroma of marijuana to the graveyard breeze and looking dejected from the loss of their generous and fiery idol, the women who came to visit their dead in nearby plots started to complain. "There's a bad crowd out there," they'd say.

That Saturday, the cops stayed a good distance away, pretending not to see us, as if they had grown used to our presence. We had a beer, smoked a joint, and went back home after Alfredo Srur took the first photos of what he'd eventually turn into a long photo essay.

WE LEFT THE cemetery through one of the side gates. Tincho, with long hair, sharp features, and nose flattened to one side like a withered leaf, took my arm and bent it behind me, forcing me into a headlock and lifting my feet an inch or two off the ground. As though creating his own reality-based film, a nonfiction reenactment of his best performance, he was playing the thief and putting me in the role of hostage.

"We're taking hostages!" he called out, pushing me toward the cemetery exit with his knee.

Chaías, Pato, and Alfredo laughed at the show.

"Call the reporters, tell the news!" Chaías egged him on.

"Don't move, asshole—you're dead!" Tincho spat in my ear. "Cameras, you piece of shit! Bring the cameras and call the judge!" he ordered an imaginary mediator.

The drug habit that Tincho picked up when he was twelve has left more than just physical scars: it has also affected the way he thinks and plans and left him with a dependency on crime that's nearly impossible to break because he has no other way to pay for his habit. As he leans against a wall in the San Francisco slum for hours just talking, half-watching the dusty pitch nearby where there's a Sunday pickup game in progress and across the street a group of kids downing beer as if it were the fountain of eternal youth, his drug habit seems a minor detail, only haphazardly connected to the conditions that led a young kid, lost between the streets and the disused railcars near Retiro station, to start on the path of robbery. Stealing, as Tincho saw it back then, was simply a trick inherited from one of his older brothers that consisted of slipping his small hand through the driver's bars on the buses at the end of the line and making off with the coins when the drivers weren't looking. "We're twelve siblings. My ma is on her own, and when I was ten I had to go out to do whatever I could. After a while, I learned how to use a gun. You can learn anything—the key is getting the other guy to believe you're bad," he told me the day I met him, running his hand through his long hair, then running the tip of his finger along the ruined bridge of his nose, its breaks reading like a map of his delinquency.

More than six months had gone by since that Saturday when Tincho played at using me as a human shield, putting me in the role of his victims, and demonstrating that—in spite of our growing closeness, the peculiar relationship we built up with my questions and his answers—I remained a potential target since I still had a few pesos in my pocket. Meanwhile, they were still exiles and willing to take from others at whatever cost just to save themselves a few more hours, even if it meant risking the rest of their lives or making a move that could send everything straight to hell. Tincho, with his arms around my shoulders, messing with me affectionately, guided me toward the exit of the cemetery where Frente is only one of many friends buried, felled by the cops' bullets or an avenging shot after some ridiculous argument with a smart-mouth from the slum. "We're all going to end up here. When I come here, I'm always visiting kids. And I always think, Where will I end up when my time comes?"

SABINA TOLD ME on the phone: "A kid from the slum tried to mug me last night." She had been on her way home, enjoying the warmth of the summer evening as she strolled hand in hand with Ricardo, the man she'd fallen in love with after those marriages from years ago that she'd been forced to flee. The little blond kid stopped them in the middle of the road. He was holding a long-barreled revolver with both hands. He pointed it at her and asked for whatever money she had on her: a mugging for ten pesos, twenty at best.

"Son, don't you know me? I'm Sabina, Frente's mom," she managed to say, fearing he would shoot without even meaning to.

It was Brian. His pupils were dilated from all the glue he'd sniffed and all the Rohypnol pills. He looked her over twice more before he realized who he was holding up. When he saw her face, even though he was drugged out of his mind, his knees hit the cement and he started to cry.

"I'm sorry, ma'am, I'm so sorry," he pleaded, his hands held up as if he were praying, though he still hadn't let go of the loaded .32.

"It's all right, Brian, take it easy. Easy there, it's all gonna be OK.

"Please forgive me," he said, still sobbing.

Sabina convinced him to lower the revolver, and he went off with his head down, mumbling incomprehensible apologies, the gun seeming to vibrate in his shaking hand. The insanity brought on by the pills had led him to try to mug the mother of the saint of young crooks, though he was so far gone he was barely aware of the sin he was committing. Sabina told me about it, worried about the kids who were now the same age her son was when he died—the ones trapped by addiction, desperate to get the money necessary for another hit even if it came only at the point of a gun, just hoping never to come down from the euphoric state they could reach through that signature mixture of pills and wine. When I first arrived at the San Francisco shantytown, I found out about those pills from Chaías and Tincho: one long afternoon they explained to me how the "rochi," as they call them, make you feel. Back then, each pill cost one peso. "If you take one, you feel it. Two, and you gotta watch yourself, man. After the third, you're not yourself any more. And by the time you remember, you might have gotten yourself beat up and you'll only realize the next day."

BRIAN KNEW VÍCTOR Vital from a distance. He was one of the kids who would come to ask Frente for yogurt whenever he showed up at Pupi's store. Under the influence of Rohypnol, Brian might have forgotten some of the rules of the slum, but not what it meant to mess with Frente's mother. Frente's generosity, his constant spending on others, would be nothing if it weren't rooted in the bravery he and his gang displayed during memorable events, recalled every once in a while by the slum's endless storytelling. One famous story is about the night he thought someone had killed his mother, and the revenge he took.

Manuel was coming back from robbing the supermarket under the stairs of the nearby apartment blocks, opposite one of the dealers in the 25 de Mayo slum.

"Hey, someone shot at Frente," said a kid on a bike.

"No!"

"Yes! They took off in a car," the kid said, pedaling away across the empty lot that doubles as a soccer field.

Manuel and the two guys he was with quickly hailed a cab, got in, and directed the driver toward Víctor's place, slamming the doors shut as the car accelerated. It turned out it wasn't Víctor who had been shot, but Sabina. Manuel found Víctor in the doorway of his shack, firing his gun wildly into the air as though he wanted to satiate his hatred. He thought his mother was dead—the bullet had entered close to her heart. The boyfriend of one of the girls he was seeing around that time had driven by the shack firing a nine-millimeter pistol, still angry after an earlier shoot-out between him and Frente that hadn't managed to settle their dispute. Sabina was eating inside, and the bullet penetrated her lung. She felt a burning sensation and saw the blood spreading across her white blouse. Sabina likes to show off the bullet that missed her heart by an inch, passing through her left lung and remaining in her body ever since, lodged next to her spine, as if her skin had stopped it millimeters before it emerged. "Here, feel it," Sabina said to me one after-noon as we were walking through the slum, raising the back of her T-shirt to show the small lump made by the bullet still stuck there.

A neighbor took her to the San Fernando hospital. Víctor arrived at the house after she had left, and from the description of the wound they gave him, he was sure she was going to die.

"Come on, let's go!" Manuel ordered Víctor when he saw him firing into the air.

"No, no, leave it!" Frente resisted, clinging to his sawed-off shotgun.

"What are you doing, you asshole?!" Manuel yelled at him. "Don't waste your bullets. Save them and let's go!"

"Huh, what? Where are we going?"

"Let's go!"

Their friend Mera appeared, having heard the gossip in the alley. He oc-casionally took part in their holdups. He was carrying two .32-caliber guns and a rifle. As they were walking toward Pollo's place, where they knew they could stock up their arsenal, a car was parking close by. They didn't even think twice: it was just what they needed.

"All right, get out. Don't worry—we won't be long," they said to the driver, who handed over the keys of the battered old Peugeot 504 before they even pointed a gun at him.

"Let me sit in front—they don't know me," Manuel said to Víctor.

"No, let me, I'll go," Víctor said.

By now they were carrying a handgun, the shotgun, two .32-caliber revolv-ers, a short .22, and a rifle. "There were four of us with those guns, because the driver actually stayed in the car. We would shoot with one, then another, until we used up all our ammo."

The appearance of their car must have seemed like a fatal omen to the kid who had targeted Víctor's house that afternoon, seeking revenge for his girlfriend's rumored betrayal.

Manuel, Víctor, and the others kept moving, not caring about whatever defense was being prepared.

"Stop the car here," Manuel said to Ernesto, who was at the wheel.

"I'm staying inside," he responded.

"I'll cover you with the .32 when you get back," said Mera.

Víctor, Manuel, and Facundo got out of the car. As they walked, they kept their guns pointed at the ground until they were three yards from the sidewalk, with the timber shack in front of them—a failsafe target for shooting practice. One of them said:

"All right. This is the car, and that's the house. This guy's done for!"

They raised their weapons and took aim.

Larry, their target, saw Frente's outline through the curtains.

"On the floor! Get down on the floor!" he shouted to his girlfriend and her friends, his kids, and his mother, who had been humming cumbia tunes at the back of the shack.

"With Facu and Víctor, we started out with the handgun: *bang, bang!*" says Manuel. "Then with the shotgun, *bang, bang!* Then with the pistol: *bang!* The driver wanted to leave when we started shooting, but Mera stopped him: 'Hey, asshole, these guys are with me!' We blew through one clip and then another—we basically destroyed this guy's house. But then we ran out of bullets. Luckily, Mera was in the car. We ran back to the car holding our empty guns, and he covered us from the car to make sure they wouldn't shoot us in the back—*bang, bang, bang!*—until we got out of there to go look for more bullets because we'd run out. We got into the car and came here, got more ammo, then cruised around a bit before returning, circling around the back via Yoli's mom's taxi stand. We shot that up, too: we didn't leave a single taxi intact."

The one who suffered most from the shoot-out, which ended up having no victims, was Pedro, a kid from the hood whose car was parked too close to the taxi place. The shotgun blasted through the driver's door of his car and left a hole as big as a skylight.

"Hey, Frente, look what you did to my car! Look at the door! Frente, you shit! Look at my door!" Manuel laughs drily as he tells the story.

"Well, that's what you get for parking there," Frente told Pedro once everything was settled. Everyone burst out laughing.

"As if just because it was Pedro's car we weren't going to shoot, eh! We weren't about to stop for anything. Even if it was Pedro's car—anyone's—whoever. We didn't care."

THAT SATURDAY WHEN things got out of control with Brian, we were heading to the cemetery in a cab. The kids asked the driver to put on Leo Mattioli, a romantic cumbia singer whose songs they all know by heart. On the way, Pato talked about Sabina getting mugged and the other things Brian had screwed up that week. Chaías recounted his own run-in with Brian and the Sapitos when they had put a gun to his sister's head.

"If it hadn't been for the guys on our block who came to her rescue, they might have killed her," he exaggerated.

He tried to take his revenge, but he couldn't get his shit together. He couldn't do without the small bag of glue he always had in his pocket, poking out like a plastic tongue with a pervasive stink. He used to smell like glue all the time, even though he was extremely careful about it: he spent all his time brushing his teeth and showering so that Sabina and his dad wouldn't find out. Whenever I was with Chaías on the way to Frente's and he was high, he'd try to appear sober. Twice he took aim at Sapo, the gang leader, firing at him from the corner while Sapo stood midway down the block, but he missed wildly both times.

"That kid hasn't got long to live," said Pato, like a doctor diagnosing a terminal illness.

Before going home, Pato agreed to try for the umpteenth time to convince Mauro, Frente's mentor, to give me an interview. We stopped outside his house, around the corner from the heart of the slum. I had tried several times through Sabina to get him to agree to an interview, to tell his own story and that of his protégé, but he had always wriggled out of it, postponing it until a future time, a moment when remembering might not be so painful. When I first saw him, he was recovering from a peritonitis operation that had left him on the brink of death; he was HIV positive, and the surgery had caught him with low immunity. I'd seen him only once at Sabina's, but all he said was that he got deeply sad talking about Víctor, that it made him feel weak, and that I should be skeptical of people who claimed they'd been close to the idol. "Now all those jerks say they went out stealing with him, hung out with him, were his best friends," he complained. When Pato and I got to his place, we couldn't talk to him—he was busy looking after his wife, Nadia.

"We can't see him right now—his wife is having a panic attack. Her little brother stole a bike from their neighbor, a little girl. It sounds like he put a gun to her head, and the girl's father just came around to complain about it. Now Nadia can't stop crying."

When Pato described what had happened, I understood how it all fit together. Mauro was married to Nadia, Brian's sister. She was the fourth daughter of a working-class couple with eight children. Brian is the youngest of the lot. Nadia was twenty-four and thin; that day, she was wearing jeans and a white tank top. As soon as we parked the car, we saw her rush out and burst into tears in front of a man who was waving his arms and miming pulling out a gun. We watched cautiously from a distance. Pato filled us in on what was going on. Later, we found out that Brian was driving Nadia crazy.

"Brian is the only boy left of the three. The oldest was ambushed by the police. The other one killed a 'rat,' a local kid, with a shot to the back of the head. Brian's the only one left," Pato said as he headed off toward his place, three blocks away.

We ended up in Sabina's house, always a peaceful space. The baby of the house was crawling about with her toys, and Pato was sipping a cold beer. I don't even remember what I was doing when we heard shots that were way too close. They were almost at the doorway, on the other side of the blue curtain that separated us from the street. Alfredo Srur ran in from the alley as if blown in by a hurricane. I knew he was a brave guy, with not only a talent for photography but also a kind of suicidal instinct that allowed him to walk through any minefield as if it were a walk in the park. Perhaps because he had been deported from California when he was eighteen and had spent a week in a camp for "illegals" in Miami, Alfredo behaved almost like he'd been inside. But that afternoon I saw him turn pale, his face becoming no more than eyes and the corners of a mouth. We didn't know whether to throw ourselves to the floor or run to the bathroom at the back of the shack. I thought about the bullet Sabina still had lodged in her back: it had come in through that very same window. The hole left by the nine-millimeter bullet is still there, right in the center of one pane, crisscrossed with tape, the size of a peephole. Frente must have been looking on as his hood shot itself to pieces.

We gathered by the door. Some ten yards away on General Pinto Street, Brian was shouting and spitting, spewing insults:

"Assholes! Shitheads!"

Brian wanted to kill Rana, a kid from the block

"You beat up my friend!" Brian shouted at Rana.

Rana had been in an argument with one of the Sapitos. Brian emptied his clip at him, but his aim was hopeless. All the neighbors rushed out, armed with their own guns, and Brian retreated as soon as he saw the dozen or so armed men coming toward him. Among them was Rodolfo, the quiet neighbor who'd been fixing an engine but who now was aiming two revolvers straight at Brian. In the middle of the street, Brian continued jumping up and down like a maniac, beating his chest:

"Assholes! Snitches! I hate you!"

The men advanced, some with handguns, three of them with sawed-off shotguns. In the background, the women were shouting to their men—their husbands, brothers, sons—as if they were at a boxing match, calling for them to land a blow or a punch, or to throw in the towel and save their own skins.

"Rodolfo! Be careful, Rodolfo!"

"Don't kill him—he doesn't deserve it, the little shit. Rodolfo, watch out! Enough!"

And so on.

"I'll kill him! I'm going to kill him!" the men raged.

One ran toward Brian; the others followed. It took two seconds. I was watching from the back of the crowd. I had crouched in an awkward position, hidden behind the blinds and curtains, peering through the cracks like a coward, determined to cling to life. Fascinated by what was going on outside, I glanced at Alfredo Srur, who looked as bewildered as I was. We both felt stupid for being so afraid while everyone else was reacting with apparent calm.

I couldn't count how many there were, or even attempt to. I had been in a few hostage situations—once on the ground behind a police car, another time half a block away from the SWAT team gathered on a roof. I assumed, given the profusion of projectiles—a mix of sounds from many different caliber bullets—that we were very close to the action. Then, suddenly, I heard a faint voice—almost a whisper—saying something like "shaking." I looked down at my hands to see if my fear was so extreme that someone felt the need to call it out. There was no denying I wasn't calm, but I wasn't trembling either. I was too caught up in what was happening to run away—not that I could have.

"Shaking," I heard again in my ear.

Ashamed, I turned around to see who it was, convinced I had shown myself to be a coward.

"I'm shaking," he said.

It was a little kid, maybe six years old. The younger brother of Manuel, Javier, and Simon—Matilde's youngest son. I was right at the back, behind the old people, the women, and even the children. The women were shouting, but I could only manage to watch.

"Don't worry," I said to the kid. "It's nearly over."

BUT THE SKIRMISH outside had only just started. The men ran directly toward Brian but then stopped short, as if still working out their plan as they went along. Brian was spinning the .32-caliber revolver on one finger and grabbing his crotch with his other hand, taunting them from a distance. The Sapitos had his back, covering him with more powerful guns even as more and more neighbors joined the crowd facing the San Francisco dealers, just out of range.

"Assholes! Fuckers!"

Brian was laughing.

They tried to work out how far off his head he was. One of the neighbors shot in Brian's direction, and he looked like he might be about to topple over, but then his gang members came to his defense, covering him from behind with a .32 and a .38.

"Guilleeee! Guilleeeee!"

A woman's scream told us someone was wounded.

FASTER THAN ANY professional emergency service, the men picked up Guillermo Rivas, his head bathed in blood. One woman jumped into a car, revved the ignition, and reversed in a screech of rubber. She opened the right back door, and the men placed the wounded man in the car like practiced paramedics. Guillermo's wife got in beside him, and they left, the car spitting gravel as they headed toward the San Fernando hospital's emergency room.

Rodolfo, the wounded man's brother, was walking in circles, guns clutched in both hands. The back of his shorts was stained with blood.

"They hit you from behind, Rodo," I joked.

"It's nothing, it's nothing," he said.

The men were handing each other fistfuls of bullets as if they were sweets. The shooting didn't stop.

Brian kept on jumping around, shouting threats, and beating his chest for another hour. His cheek was bleeding—he had hit himself as he spun the .22. In the end, though, he wasn't destined to die that day—it was just a brush with death.

There were more shots, many more, but nobody thought of calling the police. Finally, I spoke to Sabina and convinced her that it would be better if they took him away and beat him up in the police station rather than letting him die like this, asking to be gunned down.

Police cars surrounded the slum, but no one came forward to say where Brian and the Sapitos were hiding.

"I'm no snitch! God is great and He will punish him," Guillermo's mother was shouting.

Not even her children could convince her to give Brian and the Sapitos away, to say they were hiding in the same shack where Víctor Vital was murdered, a shack that was now home to a group of women loyal to the Sapitos. The rest of the neighborhood sees the Sapitos as lowlife rats who "wouldn't recognize their own mothers when they're on those pills" and who steal without regard to class or codes, without the rules that existed when Frente was alive, taking from those who had the most and giving to those with the least. The cops found them eventually, but it was ten at night by the time things calmed down.

WE WENT BACK on Tuesday around lunchtime. Rodolfo was on his doorstep again. He had a bullet wound on his butt—they had shot him with a .38 and the bullet was still inside. He pulled his pants down to show me the perfect round hole it had made. Half an hour later, Guillermo came out of the house. He had a scar like his brother's now on his left cheek, a bit smaller, from a .32. The bullet had entered his face near his right eye. According to the doctors, it was still lodged there. When they got together to look at the X-ray, they exclaimed in amazement that it was just a millimeter from his brain. They didn't call it a miracle in the hospital. They said, "You're more than lucky—you've won the jackpot!"

It seemed like the zone of protection Frente offered had widened—he'd always been invoked to protect young gang members from the police, but now it seemed that he could sway bullets from people in the hood, too. Frente, who began by stealing expensive bikes from athletic rich people in the capital, now had to save his own people from a new war. That's how they immediately saw things in the hood: as the beginning of the war Frente had tried to avoid by imposing respect on the slum while he was alive. That evening, he had been called on to save—among others—Brian, who was a thief through and through, just like Frente had been.

7

With time, Daniel's body grew accustomed to his small bed in the intensive care unit. One day, he was no longer connected to the machine that helped him breathe. On another visit, the helmet of white bandages that had protected the enormous wound on his head was gone. The childish fluff on his upper lip thickened, and Matilde let these tiny signs of life sustain her hope that he would someday recover. His sister Estela felt hopeful when she discovered that if she touched his right hand, he sometimes moved the left one ever so slightly. They continued to search his face for an alert expression. But gradually, the family came to accept this state of death in life, the abysmal emptiness of their loved one, who, according to medical experts, would never awake from his coma. Daniel lay in intensive care with his entire body intact except for his caved-in head, a cruel reminder of the sickening moment when his head hit the post, the blow that had shocked Javier and all of the cartoneros crammed into the train car. "His brain obeys him on one side, but not the other, where the wound is. He'll live until his heart gives out," was the verdict from Marga, the mai, weeks after the accident. We were seated at her kitchen table, and she was speaking to me about her life, no longer inhabited by the spirit of the African woman whose presence gave her the ability to speak Portuguese.

"Marga, you had a ceremony for him, but he's still in bad shape. Will he die?"

"Now is not the moment. It will happen when God wills it to happen. We all come into the world with a mission. I'm old, and it could be that I'll live a long time yet, because I came to suffer, to cry, to laugh. But some children arrive and are so pure that when their time comes . . . I believe in reincarnation. There are kids who die young because that's all the time they came with. We all have our time."

In Marga's world, everything has a religious explanation. The paradox is that her role, the mandate she carries on her wrinkled skin like a tattoo, obliges her to help even those people from the slum who seek to change their destinies, using pagan practices to plead with the saints of her religion. In Daniel's case, Marga went into battle on his behalf, her body possessed by the spirit of the African woman in a ceremony to Ogún: it was the night of the cleansing, when the air was thick with perfume and she broke candle after candle as she rolled them over my back. Matilde had stolen the yellow chicken Marga requested, and then the mai had offered its warm blood to Ogún. Some weeks later, she spoke to me about the difference between Daniel, a cartonero from age seven, and his brothers Javier, Manuel, and Simon, thieves who had escaped from jails and lockups so often they had all lost count. That Manichean vision, where the good pay for the bad, is the same belief that Matilde confessed to me one September afternoon in the old bar around the corner from the San Fernando hospital. "I think about how my boys faced all those gunshots and the one who was different somehow paid on their behalf. Maybe that's why the other three are still alive. I feel God is punishing me for them. Somehow, it's not possible that they've escaped all of their scrapes unscathed—someone always has to pay. And an innocent paid. The innocent always pay for the sinners."

Marga also has a dead son, Miguelito, an innocent who never stole but who paid for his brother's sins. Marga's eldest son, Cachito, is still in Olmos prison for stealing a car. As the heir to a family with a rich criminal history, he feels responsible for the police shoot-out in Beccar that ended the life of the best among them. "I should have been the one brought back home shot dead the way he was," Cachito would tell his mother, racked with guilt. Although Miguelito was eighteen when he was killed, Marga remembers her murdered son as though he were a child. "He was small. He was always with me—wherever I went, he came along. And the police killed him for no reason. He hung out with good people, he came home early when he went out dancing, he was a great soccer player—they called him "Leftie"—that's why everyone knew him and loved him." Marga doesn't recount the details of his death, but she's sure it was an "evil" killing. The police told her that they shot him for being a "criminal" as he and another kid were escaping in a car. "How could you shoot him if my son had never been arrested, not even for not having his ID?" she asked the police inspector in the only discussion they ever had about it.

Everyone used to tease Miguelito for being such a mama's boy. Like most thieves, his older brother didn't want the youngest of the family to get involved in crime. "Mom, don't let him run around on the streets so much," Cachito would tell Marga. Even when Miguelito got the chance to go to the beach at Mar del Plata with his school, his mother wouldn't let him go—she was too afraid. "Maybe God punished me for giving the other son more freedom," Marga believes, just like Matilde.

Not that she gave him that much freedom. In actuality, Cachito would escape and she would go out looking for him, dragging him and his friends back to the house with the large yard and winding vines that sat opposite the soccer field and the slum. Cachito belonged to the same clan as Mauro, Frente's grandfather. Marcelo and Fernando, who was murdered, were also part of the group, as were Camerún, who was killed by the police, and a kid with the last name of Sejas, who died of AIDS. "They were all the same age, and they were all part of the street band Los Cometas de San Fernando."

Street bands and Umbanda cropped up time and again over the course of the afternoon as we spoke about kids who were now dead, boys who had been together through years of carnivals. It was only toward the end of my session with Marga, this mai who had avoided me, remaining in the shadows despite her centrality to the tales of crime in the hood, that I managed to connect the story of Miguelito, her son who was murdered by the police, with the stories I'd been told as soon as I entered Frente's territory one winter's day in 2001. That morning, a much loved and respected character in the hood, Roberto Sánchez, who went by Pupi, sought us out, intrigued. Squinting into the low sun, he grimaced under his long, well-kept hair and asked me, the photographer, and the driver what had brought us to the slum.

"Frente's story?" Roberto knew Frente Vital from when he'd been a little kid and they used to beat him up to chase him off the corner, which in those days belonged to the older generation of thieves. He told me to meet him at his place that afternoon. "I want to show you my list," he said. "Here, in these few blocks, more than twenty kids have died that I know of. I wrote down all of their names. I keep the full list at home." His home is a wooden shack where, amidst the meager surroundings, he has collected piles of souvenirs of life in the slum: pictures torn from magazines, posters, photos, and more. He showed me his evidence: fourteen pages of notebook paper, handwritten in neat capitals, filled to the margins. "Here I counted all the deaths. Far too many of them." Listed on the pages were the names of the fallen, followed by their nicknames underlined in pen.

Roberto also showed me photographs, newspaper cuttings, and police reports with images of bodies lying on the asphalt. Almost all of the victims were young kids. He has one picture of Los Cometas de San Fernando: thirty kids piling on top of one another, spreading their arms to show off their fuchsia-colored costumes, arms open, smiling for the camera. Few of them are still alive, Roberto told me. You could tell the whole story just from that photo—recounting each individual's story, one by one, you could learn about all the bloodletting that happened in the San Francisco slum in the 1990s. That story is also in written form in Roberto's list. He couldn't help but record the deaths. He started his notes when the first kid died—he didn't write much, just a few lines about their appearance: eye color, features, and a few other details, such as the way they died, the circumstances of their death. He'd never shown his notes to anyone before, but that day he gave me the originals, just asking me to make sure I brought them back. "Do what you can with them," he said, letting go of those deaths as if concluding his tribute.

Roberto's document begins with an introduction and a summary:

This is a small tribute I would like to offer to all my friends who died from police gunfire. Some chose to commit suicide, others died accidentally, and still others were the victims of street fights. Nine of them died on the streets of my hood, where they played as children. The streets are: French and General Pinto, where I live, as well as Las Tropas, Sarratea, Berutti, and Quirno Costa. Of all the kids named here, the majority were part of the community of young thieves of our time. But not all of them were crooked. The two girls I name in this tragic history weren't involved in anything, but fate decreed that one should die in an accident and the other by suicide, both with firearms. I think a lot of this had to do with unemployment, bad company, lack of affection, the misery that exists in these ghettoes, and above all something that is devastating our society: drugs that destroy you mentally as well as physically. Many of the kids shot by the police were drunk or high. Some of them I grew up with, others I watched grow up. My god, they were too young to die! Some weren't even twenty years old. Most of them stopped by my place from time to time—I run a small store. They bought beer and soda, they sat on the bench on the sidewalk and drank peacefully. Some of the ones I name below didn't die in our hood, but nearby, in Tigre, General Pacheco, Virreyes, Don Torcuato, and, of course, San Fernando. Of my twenty-five friends who tragically lost their lives, fourteen were part of Los Cometas de San Fernando, of which I am also a member. They were excellent companions, despite the poor choices they made. There are also many who were wounded by bullets, some ending up maimed or disabled. Others are serving time. Still others are back on the streets after serving their sentences. Yes, I know, it sounds like the Wild West, but all this happened in my hood, in the 1980s and '90s. Here are names and surnames, exact dates, and twenty-five graves waiting for a flower. Here are the names and nicknames of those who lost their lives, and the details of how.

Reading his long and thoughtful text, the succession of fallen kids makes your stomach clench, blurs your vision, and becomes unbearable. Of all of those deaths, the one that moved me most was Camerún's.

His real name was Fernando Vargas, and like all the kids who take a wrong turn, he began with small-time theft and then moved on to more valuable hauls. When he tried drugs, though, he couldn't stop anymore. His family went out with a cart and horse collecting stuff to recycle. He did, too, until he got himself into some bad company, and that was that. From small stuff, he went on to steal cars. He would drive around the hood in a different car every day. He was darker skinned than most, with straight hair, narrow eyes, and a smile peeking at the corners of his mouth. He knew how to show respect, and in turn he was respected by his friends. He liked to dress well—leather jackets and new pants and sneakers. I think that's because when he was a kid he went half-naked and barefoot. As he grew older, he'd go out stealing when he was high. One time they shot him in the back, but he was saved by being high on pills. That kept him alive. Lots of kids around here were injured like that, by the police or in street fights, and all the nine or ten who spoke to me said the same thing: they felt a strong blow when the bullet hit, but they were able to keep moving. They said that what saved them from passing out was the alcohol and drugs they had inside them, which gave them the strength to stay on their feet. In the hood there were—and still are—those damn police moles, snitches. In this case it was a woman who betrayed Camerún. The whole place knows she works with the police. The patrol car would stop by her place daily—that was where the guys in charge of the streets would meet with the corrupt cops. One day Camerún stole a car in a hood called Infico, full of apartment blocks, and an unmarked cop car followed him. He spotted them and sped off, but they caught up with him and riddled him with bullets on the highway to Tigre. During the vigil, the family opened the casket and we saw that they'd blown half his face away with a shotgun.

Roberto's prose is relentless. It is repeated with each death: Camerún, Papilo, Taty, Poti, Samuel, Cuervo, Laly, Fredy, Gorda María Marta, Chinito, Maikel, Miki, Miguel "the tall one," and Miguelito, the mai's son who wasn't into stealing. "The story of Pupi is the story of my eldest son—the one who's locked up—and his gang. There was a security guard on French and Ituzaingó, and this guard's son—they called him Fredy—he killed other kids, a whole bunch of them. On the corner where Pupi lived there was a store. That was where Manco died. The ones who didn't die there are still around, but Fredy disappeared from the slum."

The San Francisco mai lists the fallen kids of the shanty. She says that if she tried to tell me each one's story, there wouldn't be enough evenings to do them all justice. But she always comes back to her dead son. There is a before and after moment in her life, a break that happened some thirty years ago. That would be Miguelito's age now—thirty—and that's how long Marga has been a part of Umbanda.

They baptized the boy into the religion at six on the evening of April 23, the day of Saint George, or—his Umbanda version—Ogún.[1] "The *pai* crossed him with blood," Marga told me. As time went by, the religion took over her life. Now, the altar to her African and Brazilian deities takes up half her home, and not a day goes by when she doesn't get a request from someone in the community. Suddenly, listening to her, I understand that she's the memory of the slums, the keeper of the most secret sins. Take Chaías,

---

1 Ogún is an Orisha, Loa, or Vodun spirit.—Trans.

who asked her to counter the spell that makes the skin on his scalp flake off but whose wish was also tied up with his love and hate for María, who was forever in love with Frente and who forbade him to see his children. In each ceremony, you can find a love story, a bitterness, even a death. After all, it is Maria who has made offerings to pai Ogún every Thursday afternoon in the empty lot facing the Pan-American Highway, praying that her children will not be struck by bullets.

The way she got into it, Marga remembers, was by visiting pai Atilio in Martínez when her eldest was sick with a virus. Atilio was a good guy. Emilia's godfather, who knew him from carnivals, introduced them. Atilio belonged to the carnival group Los Fifí de Victoria, and Marga always loved carnival. They struck up a friendship just before Miguelito was born; the pai wanted to be his godfather. Marga's husband, a tango singer with a taste for wine and womanizing, was leaving her on her own more and more often. "He spent all his time in bars and treated me badly." He had another woman, a blonde he saw for years. That April, they baptized Miguelito in the religion, and in June, when he was five months old, the tango singer left her. She was alone and unemployed. But the godfather who had introduced her to Atilio had a diner in Martínez, on Edison Street, so she started there as cook. A little while later, though, her friend expanded the business and began to put on singing and dancing to appeal more to a nighttime crowd, and her tango singer ex-husband turned up as a star performer, always with the other woman in tow. Marga couldn't stand it, so she quit and got a job in a restaurant in Tigre, where she felt independent. Soon, apart from the daily grind, religion became the most important thing to her. "That was my life: working and seeing pai Atilio. Although I hadn't yet been baptized, I worshipped the pai gods, cleaned the temple, went to the ceremonies."

Miguelito was seven when Marga decided that she wanted to fully join the religion. It wasn't Atilio who baptized her, but a mai. "I met her because she had a kid we befriended, a guy who grew up in my house. Now he's dead, too. We all called him 'Aunty Rina.'" Aunty Rina's real name was Daniel, according to his ID. He ran away from a home where he wasn't allowed to express his sexuality and spent more time with Marga, the abandoned woman, making himself indispensable, becoming her best helper and closest confidant. Marga worked in the restaurant while he looked after Emilia, Jorge, and Cachito. When she got back, Aunty Rina had cleaned, cooked—nobody could beat his rice and bread puddings—and he'd have the three kids washed, ready for dinner around the kitchen table, and then to bed. "My children adored him: with them he was like a mother hen. He was struck down suddenly four years ago by AIDS." Aunty Rina had belonged to the Umbanda religion since childhood. He began to talk to Marga while they cleaned or washed clothes together, about the possibility of her becoming a mai, committing to the religion, putting her body in a trance, letting the spirits take her over. . . . "Now I have my temple and my things, and I have children who I also baptized into the religion. It's a chain. The mothers have children, and so they pass on the religion. It's only when you become a mai that you can start having children."

Just like Matilde, Marga has a mole tattooed on her left cheekbone. At sixty-five, she still laughs over that moment of complicity, of adventure, the statement she made at just sixteen years old. There were three of them, friends who were just starting to explore their freedom, going out with their first boyfriends, walking arm in arm down the streets, feeling giddy at the life spreading out before them. Marga was an agile girl with long legs who loved to play basketball and was studying dressmaking. That night, once the inky pricking on their faces was finished, they looked at each other and then immediately went and got drunk. Soon afterward, Marga began to meet the thieves who were all around her. "I got to know the delinquent kids," she says with a proud smile. Her connections with the underworld in the northern suburbs are like badges of honor on her path to becoming a mai. One of her brothers was among the first inmates of Olmos prison. Luis "Gordo" Valor, the head of the most famous gang of the 1990s, grew up two blocks from her house and is godfather to one of her nieces. "I was a woman surrounded by crooks," she says. Her uncle was a smuggler and thief who crossed the Plate River running all kinds of goods depending on the season. Through her relatives, she ended up going out with a member of the Rififí gang: there were seven of them, sharply dressed in black turtlenecks and always carrying briefcases. When they got out of their shiny limo in the San Isidro shopping mall, the whole block trembled. "Back then, agreements were respected," Marga said. "If the police said, 'This is our turf,' then they would go and rob somewhere else, no problem."

The police and their blue shadow always turn up in even the most innocent slum story. Even if they aren't the ones doing the killing, they're there, refusing to intervene to help the little guy in a place where the strongest is always the one in charge. The police are so omnipresent that they even appear in religious accounts. All the keenly devout kids had told me already, and now the mai confirmed it: the patron saint of the young gang members is Saint George, or pai Ogún, according to the Umbanda religion. "Pai Ogún is our warrior, and yet at the same time, strangely, he also represents the police. We ask him for protection." I found out that the ceremony at Frente's grave is a variation on the offerings that thieves make to Saint George every few months so as not to get arrested or shot dead. Saint George is the saint worshipped all across the slums of Buenos Aires, from north to south. Saint George is the tattoo on Manuel's back, looking like one of those old, badly printed posters, and his medieval presence is imprinted on the skin of most of the kids I've met. The sharpened lance pictured in the knight's hand as he takes aim at the roaring seven-headed dragon coiled at the feet of his white horse appears inked on the bodies of young thieves. The knight is seen killing all types of infernal creatures, from fierce snakes to winged monsters.

Saint George is a myth from ancient Rome. He was born in 280 AD and died twenty-five years later, on April 23 in the year 305. His battle against the seven-headed dragon is believed to symbolize the empire founded on the seven hills of Rome. His father was a senior officer in the Roman army. His proximity to power gave young George a chance to meet Emperor Diocletian, who, impressed with the boy's bravery, asked him to join his corps. Little did he imagine that George would become a dissident—his mother had secretly brought him up a Christian. The emperor ordered violent repression of the advances being made by the monotheism professed by Jesus of Nazareth, and when George refused to take part in the persecution of Christians, Diocletian decided to have him tortured and killed. The executioners threw him naked into a pit, bound his feet and hands, beat him, dragged him through the mud, tied him to a wheel bristling with knives, then whipped him until he lost consciousness.

But the different versions of the Judeo-Christian chronicle all agree that his wounds healed miraculously, and death seemed to flee him. One of the emperor's sorcerers gave him a poisoned drink, but it had no effect on him. These apparent miracles tore the sorcerer's pagan faith to shreds. In the end, he asked George to resurrect a man who had died a few days earlier to prove the strength of his forbidden faith. George brought the man back to life with a prayer. The sorcerer told the soldiers of the miracle, and when the story reached the ears of Diocletian, he ordered that the sorcerer be beheaded. Then he sent emissaries to get George to retract his faith in return for putting an end to the torture. But it was useless.

George resisted for days. His patience exhausted, Diocletian had him dragged to the temple of Apollo. In front of the court, the priests, and the people, George again refused to worship the Roman gods. As a final act of faith, he caused the pagan statues of the temple to topple. Empress Alexandra, a beautiful woman who had hidden her true faith, jumped up from her throne and shouted to her husband and to the crowd amazed by the miracle-working prisoner: "I am also a Christian!" Diocletian, whose government was known as the "era of martyrs," had his own wife whipped to death. Then he unleashed the viciousness of his executioners on George: they stoned him and tied him to a horse that they forced into a wild gallop. After letting the horse run a full mile, they assumed George breathed no more, but the soldiers were astounded when they saw, upon approaching the body, that he had not a single wound. Finally, on April 23, his head rolled in front of the Roman crowd. It was from that day on that his miracles occurred, miracles that always happened on behalf of the needy; during his lifetime, he had spent his fortune on helping the sick and giving clothes and food to the poor and the persecuted.

The other story that forms the basis of George's sainthood is a medieval tale of fairies and enchanted lakes. Jacopo da Varazze—known in Spanish as Santiago de la Vorágine—was a Dominican friar from Genoa who, in the second half of the thirteenth century, compiled in Latin the biographies of nearly two hundred saints. According to his version, George was a Roman officer who traveled the world as a wandering knight. This was how he arrived at the city of Silebe in the province of Libya at a time when a dragon living in the depths of a lake was terrorizing the region. The inhabitants of Silebe came up with an odd strategy: they would feed two sheep to the voracious animal every day. Soon, the flocks were decimated and famine was threatening, so the king decided that to placate the dragon, they needed worthier victims. The village had a lottery from which a young virgin was chosen to be sacrificed. As luck would have it, though, it was soon the turn of the king's only daughter, a delicate, silent princess. The king protested, but the villagers were insistent, so finally he agreed to sacrifice his daughter, and the princess wept and went obediently down to the lake. They were about to hand her over to the monster when a warrior as beautiful as an angel appeared to rescue her. Saint George, spear in hand, galloped over the waters on his white charger and pierced the dragon's heart. Together, the knight and the princess dragged the dying monster up to the village to finish it off in front of the crowd.

The myth of Saint George, with its metaphor of salvation in return for the sacrifice of innocents, echoes the explanation that Marga and Matilde use to understand the tragic fates of their younger sons. Marga feels that Miguelito, murdered by the police, paid for her sins and those of her family, including her other son, who was a thief. Matilde believes that Daniel suffered the accident that left him in a deep coma because in this way the sins of his mother and his three thieving brothers, Manuel, Simon, and Javier, were paid for. Worshipping Saint George is an attempt to stop fate from taking innocent lives in exchange for these young knights without steeds who choose a life of crime as they go out to fight and steal at gunpoint.

The mai has had her own Saint George, her own pai Ogún, ever since she was baptized into the Umbanda religion. For Umbanda practitioners, the Ogúns are seven different deities, each with a different origin: Marga is the daughter of the Ogún who she says is an ancient Indian. She makes offerings to him to ask for protection for the young thieves. Marga concentrates on explaining the rites. "The kids steal and use what they get to buy everything for the tray that I prepare for Ogún. Ogún is the same person that people call Saint George. He is our warrior, and he's also the police." Perhaps owing to his origins as a Roman officer, or perhaps because he is the patron saint of the Argentinian cavalry, to the faithful, Saint George is also the police. But that doesn't diminish him or tarnish his standing: it's as if, to obtain impunity when stealing, it is necessary to negotiate with the saint who embodies the martial nature of the enemy that must be neutralized. Of course, the gifts to Ogún are always best stolen, certainly as far as the African woman is concerned. And it is always the African spirit in the mai's body who intercedes between the thieves and pai Ogún.

"How long have you been visited by African deities?"

"About twenty years. But it's only been eight years that I've been able to embody them."

"How does it work, embodying spirits?"

"You call on the spirit, and suddenly you feel as if you're floating, as if your body isn't even there. I embody pai Yangó and pai Ogún, the saint. The spirit takes over your body, your tongue, but you can see and hear everything that's going on. You're talking to another person, and the spirit is using my mind and my eyes and can see everything you're doing and saying, but when she departs, she leaves only what she wants in me. She can't take over my mind, because if she takes over my mind, then I die. What she wants me to know, I know, what she doesn't, I don't. For example, when my son died, five days earlier she told my daughter that they were going to cry a lot, that they should take care of me and my heart. When she told me that, I thought maybe my father was going to die—he was almost ninety at the time. We never imagined it would be Miguelito. The day they killed him, I disowned my pai: why didn't he tell me what was going to happen to my boy? When the African returned, she told my children that they had no right to talk about what they are not permitted to speak of, that they are in the power of Oaxalá, the Supreme. All the pai, even Ogún, are children of Oaxalá. Then there are the Oriyas—they're the saints. The Cosme are the babies. Mai Oyún doesn't speak, she makes the sound of weeping, and the Cosme just fight, play, and drink milk. They crawl, they don't walk, but they're the strongest because they take away the bad things from people. Here I also get a lot of women who are prostitutes, and I wash them in Pompayira because she attracts men. And then you have the Exú, who are also led by the pai Oaxalá, even though people say they are devils. They are low spirits: with them you can harm others. But they also do good things. I don't do bad things, I made a promise. I had a grandchild die more than twenty years ago, and I promised to heal the sick and the young. I separate couples or I join them, I cleanse houses, but whatever it is, I always do it for the good. I work with the Seyú, but only the good side."

The African woman, the character who takes over Marga's body, making her speak broken Portuguese, has a special predilection for stolen objects. That's why, even though there are a number of spirits that the mai takes on, it is the African woman who is in charge of putting together the array of symbolic offerings for Ogún every Thursday. "The African woman prepares the tray, and that's how she pays Ogún. First you write the name of the person for whom you're making the payment. The tray is decorated with green, white, and red crepe paper, the colors of pai Ogún. You separate an ear of corn carefully, because it mustn't be broken. You toast it on a dish, and you have to keep stirring the whole time so it doesn't burn. Then we make the popcorn. You put seven long, well-marinated rib cuts to cook in the oven, not overdone or tough. You place them in the shape of a horseshoe. You add three oranges and three apples, each cut into seven pieces. Then you just need some really fresh lettuce leaves, seven yards of green, white, and red ribbon, and a toy wooden knife. Finally, you offer up a light beer with a glass, and a cigar. It all has to be new."

One of the examples Marga commonly gives to prove how effective her spells are involves Simon. Simon escaped certain death at least twice, which for the mai means his body has a miraculous shield of protection. The first was the time he was shot in the chest in an alley in the 25 de Mayo slum, and when he got to the emergency department the nurse said to him, "God loves you." The second took place near Marga's house, on the far side of the slum, when he was holding up a supermarket. On both occasions Simon was badly wounded. But if he was protected, why did the bullets touch him at all? Marga believes that the injuries he's had in spite of the spells are the result of his being rebellious and hard headed.

The day he held up the store, Simon was at the mai's place when she was possessed by the African woman.

"Boy, don't go out. You mustn't touch your fire arms," the African woman warned him.

When she was free of the African woman's spirit, Marga insisted:

"Listen to the mai."

Simon looked at her and smiled. She went into her room to take off her ceremonial skirt, and by the time she came out, he had gone. Fifteen minutes later, she heard the shots.

"Simon!" came from her lips like an incantation.

That time, Simon took hostages. He and his partner Corcho hadn't taken into account the extra private security guard they had in the place. They wanted the main safe, but their information was wrong: they thought the money was upstairs. The police arrived while they still had the staff and the clients down on the floor. There was no negotiation: the cops rushed through the aisles with their guns at the ready, and when they realized there was somebody up above, they fired a hail of bullets into the air. They fired machine guns from beneath the wooden floorboards as if they were aiming to shoot the hidden robbers in the head. Corcho, just seventeen, fell without seeing the faces of his assassins. Simon was finally cornered between two checkout counters. He surrendered but still felt the sharp pain of a bullet entering his leg moments later, quickly followed by one of the three shots that have left deep scars on his forearm, bullets from different robberies that penetrated his flesh at almost the same point. His sister Estela was in despair when she heard the news. "They've killed him," they told her. She ran immediately to the store. Her mother, Matilde, was only a few minutes behind her, running to Simon's rescue. "Let me through—I'm his mother!" Simon had crawled out to the sidewalk, hoping to reach the street to escape being finished off. "Matilde arrived just in time. They were going to kill him, they wanted to shoot him in the head, to kill him," says the mai. "Simon has a very dark way ahead of him. Life holds great danger for him. But for me, Simon is like my own son Facundo—if I have to offer my life, if they have to kill me to save him, so be it."

"Do you think the kids are aware of the danger when they go out stealing?"

"I don't know if they're not aware of it, or if they know about it but just want to defy it. These kids haven't imagined the kinds of consequences that can come from messing around on the streets. They don't see how dangerous their way of life is. They think they're strong, that they can do anything, but it's not like that. About five years ago, back when the hard times started, the kids started stealing way too young. Ten years ago it was unheard of for the really young kids to be stealing, even if they were from a family of thieves—that's what the adults were for. But in the past few years, poverty has become so terrible, and the police get worse all the time. And then the drugs came and the kids started hanging out on the corners, shooting up. They started with pills and garbage like that. First it was the older ones who got high, then the younger kids. With those pills, they lose all sense of reality. They go crazy."

As calmly as a housewife serving maté in her kitchen, Marga tells the stories of her children and their friends, whom she began to treat like her own children, too, sheltering them in the safety of her home. "I had them cooped up in here for days when I was afraid the police would get them," she says. Her devotion to the young crooks who hung out with her now-imprisoned son, and then her grandson, also made some people in the slum criticize her: they say she's in charge of a hideout and living off ill-gotten gains.

In her house the kids found not only refuge, food, and a mattress to sleep on but also an expert in removing bullets and caring for minor injuries. Like many mothers of gang members, Marga ended up on their side, tired of fighting against these out-of-control kids, and tired of the police abuse that awaited them should anything go wrong on a job. As the mother of a grown-up thief, sister to another delinquent in large and long-standing gangs, and niece of a smuggler from the 1960s, Marga has been a refuge for the youngest generation, for the grandchildren, one that Simon still heads toward upon being released from prison and returning to the slum after two years away. And her son Cachito and his brothers served as mentors and guides for those just setting out on the path of crime. In the same way that Frente Vital learned from Mauro, a good friend of Cachito's, about the kind of honor and loyalty that were going out of fashion, so Marga's grandson Facundo, who was friends with Frente, Simon, and others the same age, looked up to his prison-hardened uncle.

"The kids saw them as role models. To Frente, no one deserved more respect than Mauro, and Facundo always admired his uncle. I would tell him off and say that he shouldn't look up to Mauro. He's my son, and it pains me to say it, but I would never have wanted this. I've worked all my life for my children—you can see it from my hands. But it hurt that my grandson idolized him, because he's such a bad example. At first his uncle wanted nothing to do with it, but after a while he was won over. Now, though, he writes to him: 'Get a grip. You have to realize that I've been locked inside for twelve years. You have to do better. I don't want any harm to come to you—you have your grandmother to look after.' They write to each other from prison. His uncle isn't happy with the life his nephew is living. He's always saying to me: 'Talk to him. Make sure that when he comes out, he doesn't go back.' Because this is the first time my grandson has been sent to an adult prison. My son says those things because he knows what it's like. He was caught a year and a bit ago, stealing a car with the owner still inside. He had just come out of prison. He was only out for six days. He came out and was caught again. Over the years, he's been in most of the prisons in Buenos Aires: he was in Sierra Chica, Batán, Dolores. The only one he hadn't been in was Campana, which is where he is now, thankfully on good behavior, and working. Before, he used to be a messenger, one of the guys who never made any effort. He says he never liked the power struggles between the inmates, what the bad cons did to keep the younger guys in their power. Where he is now, nobody takes them as husbands—that's what my son fights against. He was in the revolt at Sierra Chica, and there was a group of bad guys who were killing people, and on the other side, his group was fighting for the kids in the yards and the ones who took refuge in the church."

Facundo also had no more than a moment of freedom, seemingly destined to follow in his uncle's footsteps. After the revolt he started in prison when he heard of Frente's death, Facundo spent half a year in an open prison. When he got back onto the street, it was a much tougher place, and the corner where his gang met was nearly empty: the ones who were still alive were still locked inside. He turned eighteen at home. "And after three months, he got caught again. The street changed, but you can always find a friend. Sometimes a friend is more powerful than family," says Marga. She only rarely gets to visit him in far-off Junín, where he was put away for armed robbery for up to four years. To make thing worse, he doesn't believe in the pagan gods; he hates the religion his grandmother practices and his mother translates for when the African woman appears. "He never wanted anything to do with it. He laughs or gets angry."

And this is why, after these failures to protect her own family, Marga, the mai, now devotes herself to praying for the health of her followers, or prepares love potions to keep a man or a woman with their lover, even when one is behind the walls of a high security prison; she sacrifices yellow chickens so that Daniel's soul does not leave his shrunken body in the intensive care bed. Marga prays for him and keeps trying. And Daniel lies there in a deep sleep, showing minimal signs of life, turning into an adolescent with a peach fuzz beard, a prisoner of the intricate machines that keep him still in this world of mud, offerings, blood, and prayers.

"How was the ceremony for Daniel?"

"I prayed to Eyú to give him life in return for sacrificing the animal. This time it was the African woman who did it, because he's very young. To us, the Umbanda, until they're fifteen they're *crianças*, children. We wish child thieves didn't exist. For me, to see a fifteen-year-old kid stealing is really hard. It hurts because they do it without thinking. They want to feel strong. Do they have any notion that they may be killed?"

8

I had tried to meet with Mauro so often that I finally decided this would be my last attempt. After I had asked to meet so many times, my requests had started to border on begging and I felt intrusive and embarrassed. Over a year had passed since I'd first tried to get in touch with him through Sabina Sotello, but I was still afraid that turning up at his place again might lead to a confrontation or a major humiliation. I understood that Mauro was torn between the pain of sharing memories of his murdered friend and the pleasure he might get from reminiscing about Frente's life. There's an old rule of journalism that says, when an interview is no longer a proposal to be either accepted or declined and instead becomes a lengthy seduction and negotiation, something must be hiding behind all those words. In Mauro's case, I thought it might be something to do with his friend Víctor Vital, that maybe there had even been some kind of betrayal that might undermine the legend that had drawn me to Frente's story in the first place.

It was toward the end of September, with Daniel in the hospital and Simon allowed to leave Almafuerte every weekend, when Mauro finally invited me into his home. I had come looking for him earlier that day and found his door closed, but I had come back again in the midafternoon, and his wife, Nadia, finally answered the door.

"Mauro's asleep, but come back in a while and maybe you'll catch him after his shower. I'll tell him you came around."

When I reappeared, Mauro was just emerging from the shower he took every day at the same time.

"If you can hold on a few minutes, I just have to change his bandages," Nadia said to me.

Nadia never treated me like an outsider. Every time I tried to interview Mauro, she had been open to it. She used to call me and give me advice about how to convince him, how to try again. I soon discovered that she would be key to letting me in on the truths normally kept from outsiders.

I stayed on the sidewalk, trying not to look too out of place. By then, having been in the area before with Manuel, Chaías, and Tincho, I was already getting recognized by some of the slum's residents: the dealers or their children nodded and smiled slightly or greeted me with a thumbs-up, showing that I was not an unfamiliar sight in the neighborhood. I'd gone with the kids a handful of times to get stuff from the forbidden dealers' shacks, so I was worried that they would spot me hanging outside Mauro's place. I didn't know what to expect from his story. I was counting on taking a back seat, letting him do the talking. Of course, after a year and a half, if anything had been left out of the accounts I'd heard, it probably wasn't about Frente's saintliness or his jealous girlfriends.

Nadia came out again.

"Cristian, Mauro says you can come in."

I walked into the main room—a combined kitchen and dining room—which contained a TV that was on but muted, a makeshift eating area with a small table, and three chairs. There were also some birthday presents arranged like ornaments, a teddy bear, and a couple of photos. In the bedroom, past a narrow, lopsided door, Mauro was lying on the left-hand side of the double bed wearing gray cotton boxer shorts. His hairstyle was straight out of the 1980s, layered and with bangs—all he needed to complete the look was to prop both of his hands behind his head. Nadia sat next to him. With a bowl full of disinfectant in one hand and gauze in the other, she went back to concentrating, as she did at that time every day, on tracing the enormous scar that ran from his navel to his lower pelvis. I decided I'd better go straight into the interview, evading the sad scene by getting out my notebook and launching right into my questions. Struggling to get a feel for the rhythm of the encounter, I went back to the basics of my trade, asking:

"Why do you need to clean the wound like that?"

"It was a peritonitis operation. These two scars here were bullet wounds, well, really only one bullet—it went in here and came out here. In between, it perforated my liver. It blew a hole inside me. But the doctor told me that the liver mends itself, it's like gelatin. In December, they cut out part of my intestine."

Mauro had been the good-looking young blond boy of the slums, a popular kid who seduced Nadia with love letters after seeing her in Olmos when she went to visit her brother Toti, who was murdered by the cops a couple of years later. When Mauro got out, he pursued her persistently until finally she fell in love with him. They were trying for a baby when he infected her with HIV, although he swears he didn't know he had the virus when they met. Near the end of our interview, Nadia confessed that she had never believed him. Her version of the story is very different: as she sees it, Mauro "ruined" her. In the slums, the concept of "ruining" someone—the adjective "ruined" and the verb "to ruin"—can apply to many different things. If an adult introduces a kid to drugs or stealing, they are said have ruined them. Someone who sells pills to the kids ruins them. The person who saws off shotguns for the kids also ruins them. Whoever passes the virus to others ruins them. So, Mauro ruined Nadia's life.

Mauro was released from prison on December 24, 1996. From then on, he kept clean; he stayed away from the life he led for twenty years, almost the same length of time he spent in Los Cometas de San Fernando. He was one of the first people in the slum to start taking pills; the Rohypnol pill craze affected him as much as the scars that now permanently mark his body. "I remember when they shot me in 1987, it was the height of the 'Ropy' pills—anything went." He and a friend were coming back from a fight with the guys from Infico, the apartment blocks just streets away from the slum. "I heard a couple of shots, but I didn't think twice about them. Then I felt as if someone had shoved me, and I walked into a lamppost. I hugged the post and started to pass out." He had collapsed. Not until he hit the ground did he realize he'd been shot. In that last lucid second before he lost consciousness, he thought he was dying. Like hundreds and thousands of others, Mauro was shot treacherously in the back, the bullet zigzagging inside his body. He never found out who fired it.

Not long after recovering from being shot in the liver, he was back in prison. His fate was the same as that of most kids of his generation, including his old friend Cachito. In Olmos prison, through friendships he formed with other inmates from San Fernando, he fell in with some guys close to

Luis Valor's gang who robbed banks and armored trucks. One of them became his best friend during his interminable confinement in that prison, the most overcrowded prison in the province apart from the hellhole called Sierra Chica. Their friendship was sealed the only way one can be in prison, other than with a shank—by one person offering a proof of humanity that overcomes the conditions of permanent subjugation. After a prison party, drunk and stumbling from the "birdie"—the prison drink brewed by fermenting newspaper ink—Mauro tore his Achilles' tendon in the showers at the far end of the block. His friend came to his aid, carrying Mauro out of the showers and asking for him to be taken to the infirmary. He even looked after Mauro afterward. He had strong arms thanks to the pull-ups he practiced on a bar in their wing, and during the weeks when Mauro couldn't walk, he carried him everywhere. He was the only one who kept his word after his sentence was up. "When you get out, wait for me. I'll come find you," he said, proving his loyalty one last time.

One afternoon, he turned up in the slum looking for Mauro. He came to offer a lucrative job, one that would solve their financial problems. Mauro had spent six years and four months in Olmos for armed robbery. "I don't regret it, but if you want to get by, you have to think ahead, you have to steal with a plan to stop stealing," Mauro reflects today.

"Your family has to go back and forth to the prison to visit you, they follow you. I used to tell the kids that you have to leave some money behind when you're put away so that they can get lawyers, make a fuss, buy the things you need. If you don't leave anything, you can't ask for anything. I only left ten pesos. I was a jerk—for that and for a lot of other things."

Mauro's thinking dates back to the days when, in the corridors of Olmos and prisons across the country, if a new inmate was taken under the wing of a "dick," he'd be able to walk up and down the corridors unbothered on the arm of his protector. Those were the last days of the big gangs, in the same period when the mafia of local cops started to take over the area's criminal underworld, turning every corner—every tiny illegal activity—into a money-making opportunity for themselves.

At that time, during the 1980s and the first half of the 1990s, there was still enough room to walk between the prison bunks. In Olmos, where twenty inmates used to sleep, there are now cots for seventy prisoners. In the places where the older gang bosses strolled, these days the most vicious young guys are in charge: the average age among the more than 3,800 inmates is twenty.

"What did you learn in prison?"

"What I learned in prison is that a criminal needs to show character, whether you're a thief or a drug addict. You have to look after the hood, you have to get along with people so that they'll open the door for you when the police are on your tail. But if you're an asshole in the hood, they'll slam the door in your face. That's what I used to tell Víctor and the kids his age. Because I could see what they were doing, how they got high, that's why I told them about what happened to me, the hit I had to take to learn to survive afterward. That's what I learned from the older guys inside."

Mauro was talking from the bed. Even after five years of a difficult life together and Mauro's continuous flirting with new girls in the hood, his wife still respected and loved him. She said nothing, just making a cup of maté before returning and continuing to clean his wounds.

"How do people survive so far from the streets?"

"You lose all sense of reality. There you live in another world, feeding on fantasies. You arrange to meet others outside all the time. You live on hope. And you're in there with cops, but no guns. On the street, they have real guns and shoot at you. You don't see that inside, it's like living in a movie where you can't hear the shots. What you hear in prison are the blows, but you forget about bullets for a while, or you remember them to fantasize about how you're going to steal, and not how as soon as you're out you're going to get it, because in actuality you're a nobody. Look around you today, all the cops patrolling, all the security on the streets, it all makes robbery so much harder than before, even though they go on about insecurity. The lack of security also affects thieves. That's why, to understand what goes on outside, I spent a lot of time in prison reading magazines, watching TV. To give you an idea, when I was put away, the austral was the official currency, and when I came out, we had pesos.[1] Nadia showed me how to use the buses, because I couldn't figure out those new coin machines.

When Mauro came out of prison, he'd walk through the streets and alleys of the slum not knowing whether people he knew were greeting him out of fear or to ingratiate themselves with a respected thief who had just won his freedom. That hurt, he says. In spite of the drug haze that he sometimes couldn't control, he had tried to be a decent man, respectful of neighbors not involved in crime, but now he faced silent prejudice from others. "People are

---

1 The austral was the official currency in Argentina from 1985 to 1991, when it was replaced by the peso. — Trans.

unfair because they judge you for your past," Mauro complains, as if this is a harder sentence than being inside. "I was lucky enough to get clean," he says gratefully. And thinking it over, he concludes that he did it for his mother, when she got sick. Only then did he become aware of how time was passing; suddenly, death appeared before him with its dark, tragic truth. That's what motivated him to try to teach the younger kids like Frente that whether they were giddy with success after a good "job," like a succession of heists that left them living like boxing champs, or they were feeling down after the worst failure, they should never forget their mothers. In prison culture, your mother is more important than God. There's hardly a single inmate without the word MOTHER tattooed in capital letters somewhere on their body. "What happened to me was that I didn't appreciate her enough. In the end, when I did, I lost her. My mom was really supportive, but I didn't understand her. I caught on too late, and by the time I did, she was gone. She died of heart failure."

The guilt of not knowing how to get straight in time to appreciate the woman who had raised him, despite all the difficulties of a life of poverty and a violent father, still haunts Mauro. Just before the end, he remembers, she was subdued, worried, and he didn't know why. One of his brothers told him: "Mom is like that because she's fallen behind on her loans." Mauro had thought she was caught up on her bills because she never admitted she needed anything: what little money came in was spent helping any of her nine kids who might be in trouble. That same day, he managed to steal eight hundred pesos in small bills. When he gave the money to her, she looked happy but said: "No, son, you look after yourself." He didn't let her go on. "No, Mom, you have it." The eight hundred pesos was a reward won with the adrenaline rush that came from holding a gun. The money was from a retail store, and there were so many small bills it was hard for his mother to stuff it all in her pocket. She barely had time to spend the gift paying off her debts: she died within days.

Mauro had just returned to the hood when he met Víctor Manuel Vital— Frente. He had seen him go by, arrogant and magnificent on his shiny motorcycle, the XR100 that Sabina had given him. He was with one of the kids of his gang, shooting the breeze while he smoked a joint, when he saw Frente cross the road on the XR, well on his way to becoming a criminal.

"And who's that kid?" he asked the guy with him.

"See how he's grown up? He's Pato's brother, Víctor. They call him Frente."

He put his index finger and thumb in his mouth and whistled. Víctor braked, his skidding wheels screeching as he made a U-turn until he was close enough to extend his hand.

"This is my friend Maurito."

"Hi, how are you? I'm Víctor," Frente said politely, using the respectful form *usted* until told to do differently.

Not long after, Víctor was put away again. "What's he in for? The same as usual." Neither Sabina nor Mauro remembers exactly which robbery led him to the maximum-security institution in Mercedes, the place where they developed prison signals with Manuel to communicate from one yard to the next. That was also where María, the one most in love with him, went to visit him without anyone knowing. But Sabina does clearly remember that she was the one who put pressure on the juvenile judge in San Isidro to make sure her son did not escape again. "I was stupid. As a mother, I wanted them to cure him. I was hoping they could improve him, that he'd get over drugs and crime. Afterward I learned that they were abused inside, that it made things worse, that they were crammed in like animals, with nothing to do, with one shrink for every 150 kids, learning how to be even more delinquent." Víctor spent two weeks locked away and began to ask his mother to bring Mauro when she came to visit. They lied to the judge and the institute: they said Mauro was a cousin who came to see him from the province of Entre Rios. The psychologist who did Mauro's assessment was from Gualeguaychú. They talked about carnivals and became friends. Mauro went in to see him, and he became Frente's protector behind the walls of Mercedes.

Mauro gave him advice gleaned from his own unfortunate experiences. "I had to tell Víctor that if he wanted to get back on the street, if the psychologist said, "Go to bed at eight and brush your teeth," he had to do whatever the guy said. Talk to him, tell him you miss your family, draw pictures for him, ask him for books you want to read, magazines, all that, so they can see that you wanna get out." Víctor didn't need telling twice. He wasted no time in becoming interested in reality outside the walls of the place, in seducing the female psychologist in charge of determining whether he had the capacity to distance himself from crime and violence, and in convincing the priest at the institution that he had found God.

Sabina herself couldn't understand how her incorrigible son, whom she had tried so often to take to church, suddenly decided to get into religion. "These guys eat saints and shit devils," his mother used to say to him and his gang when they talked about their faith. The local priest also fell for Víctor's trickery. Among the activities for the incarcerated kids, the priest ran a theater group in which one of the most popular performances was Frente impersonating their teacher in his clergy robe.

In spite of the dozens of robberies Frente was accused of, he managed to get a summons to the juvenile court in San Isidro to decide his fate. "He charmed the psychologist and wrapped her around his little finger, and they ended up setting him free. After that, there was bad blood with the tough kids inside because they said Vital got preferential treatment," Sabina remembers. They let him go, but on the advice of the same psychologists, they forbid him to say good-bye to his fellow inmates: they thought it would be counterproductive for the others to see him go free. When they found out he was leaving, the others organized a protest asking to be able to say good-bye. Sabina recalls those days clearly: it was the last time Víctor was in prison, the longest stretch he spent inside.

"Was he different from the rest of the kids?" I ask Mauro.

"He was one of a kind. He went and got money and made sure everyone lived well in the slum. They were all friends, but nobody really ran with him. Two or three kids might have drifted with him for a while, but that's all."

MAURO TRIES TO clear up some of the Frente myths spread by those who claimed to be close to him, show-offs who said they'd hung out with him just to have some of his fame and bravery rub off on them. Mauro himself never went out on a robbery with Frente. The only time they were going to do something together was when they had plans to hold up a place in Pacheco that they had good information about. It was a Sunday, between seven-thirty and eight, when the employees began work. They couldn't be late. They were after the weekend's takings, and it was a matter of going in, pointing their guns, taking the money, and getting out as quickly as possible to avoid the cops from the nearby precinct. "We'll go on the motorcycle, run in, and that's it. Good money. C'mon," Mauro told him. "OK, you're on," Frente accepted. When he arrived at Pintos and French, Mauro will never forget, Víctor was with three friends, one of them Manuel, and they were still laughing and recounting how much fun they had had the night before, partying and dancing cumbia. Mauro pulled him aside and said, "Did you forget?" "Uh, shit, I forgot. I just got back from the club. I can't go like this." In those days, not being sufficiently with it to go out to a "job," especially with a respected thief like Mauro, was reason enough to back out. Mauro didn't complain. He went off to find another partner and headed out to Pacheco to carry out the plan. It was easy, he remembers. He made fifteen hundred pesos, when they were worth a dollar each. Back in the hood, before going home he passed by Frente's place to show off the loot. "See, dumbass? What you had to do was super easy." "I always laughed at him," he recalls, stretched out on the double bed, the wound on his abdomen now clean thanks to Nadia's gentle, skillful ministrations.

PACHECO, IN THE Tigre district just north of San Fernando, was one of the places where kids like Frente most often practiced their robbery skills. Mauro remembers a night when Víctor headed out with another two kids in a car, with a place already in their sights, ready to clean it out and flee. But that day they couldn't even get near it. They were going slowly, carefully, when a private security car noticed them and started following them like a dog after a bone. "It seems like they had a radio, because before they realized it, they were cornered and the shoot-out started." The three of them jumped out of the car and ran to hide in the first shack they could find in the shanty. Bad luck and telltale neighbors gave them away. Ale, a big, strong kid whom Víctor had shared time with in prison, was left with his chest exposed to the police bullets as he was trying to get to the end of the alley at full tilt, and he fell. Víctor fired from a fence, managing to halt the police advance with the burst of gunfire. That was how, according to witnesses, he reached his friend, who was lying motionless and silent as he bled to death in the mud. Frente lifted him up as if he were a fair maiden in a fairytale. "He held him in his arms and went on shooting under Ale's body." This was what several of Frente's friends had told me in what had always seemed to me to be an embellished account that I had to check out with Mauro. "That's what the witnesses said afterward. They tried to escape in the car, but the one driving lost it and crashed. They jumped out of the car. Víctor ran, Ale as well, and while they were running, Víctor heard a shout. When he turned around, Ale was on the ground. He started shooting like crazy so they wouldn't get him. They say he managed to lift him and carry on shooting. But afterward he told me Ale was already dead by the time he picked him up."

That day, Mauro was on a motorcycle he had bought with money he'd stolen as soon as he'd come out. He bumped into a kid and stopped to ask:

"Hey—you know what the guys are up to?"

"Nah, but I think they might be in some kind of trouble in Los Troncos," he said. Mauro didn't wait for him to finish.

Just as he was, half-naked in the heat, he set out for Pacheco to rescue Frente, fearing that the police in these northern districts would follow through with their threat. "I went there, but I couldn't get in because the cops were crawling all over the slum. Then I started asking, and nobody knew anything. I spoke to a local gang and told them I was friends with the kids, that they could trust me. "They killed two and arrested the others," they told Mauro. He didn't know what to do. He thought one of them was still hiding out in the slum. He sped off on his bike to get guns from San Fernando and some help to get into the alleys and check things out. "We went in, knocked on doors, talked, and some guys came out and called us over." The kid who was left was hiding in a shack but couldn't get out. Mauro gave some money to the guy he'd brought on the bike so that he could get a cab and disguised the kid who had avoided capture as best he could. "I gave him the cap and sunglasses and got him out. They already had Frente."

Those rescue missions, those adventures where someone sets out, no questions asked, in search of a friend in mortal danger, are rarely heard of in the slum these days. That solidarity between thieves is gone now, along with the kids who stole beyond the borders of their home territory. The new young thieves steal from their neighbors, not caring who they are. I finally understood this in September, some six months to the day after Brian pranced like a mad grasshopper shouting for them to kill him, and the Sapitos, to defend him against the neighborhood fury, shot Guillermo at close range, penetrating him with the bullet that miraculously stopped millimeters short of killing him or leaving him a vegetable.

As usual, it was Sabina Sotello who told me the news over the phone. This time it wasn't a fake shoot-out with the local police and their death squads in Don Torcuato, or torture in police stations, or a woman shot by the careless fire of an overexcited cop. This time it was someone shot in San Francisco on almost the same alley where Frente Vital was murdered. "They killed one of the Sapitos," Sabina told me. They had shot and killed the eldest of the brothers, the nineteen-year-old, the finishing touch to a weekend like the one six months earlier that had ended with Brian challenging twenty men who wanted to finish him off for ruthlessly stealing from children and old people. Now they had killed a Sapito, the oldest Sapo, the same Sapito who was thought to have shot Guillermo, or Rodolfo; the same Sapito who had betrayed Brian and left him on his own in the juvenile court. Of the few certainties that a gang had when the codes of honor were still respected, one was that a member wouldn't sleep with another guy's girl, and one that, when it came to testifying in court, they'd back you up even when faced with the worst forms of torture: the plastic bag over the head and the cattle prod.

Since that confrontation, Brian had been in a maximum-security institution in the city. The Sapitos had been reduced to the small alley in San Francisco where they had taken refuge six months earlier. Only minimal territory is left to pariahs like them, rats who can't walk through the shanty greeting folks because their exclusion has reached a point where they have to live confined to a few square meters, relegated to a ghetto by other people's stares. For days, the Sapitos had been high on pills and wine, stealing from anyone going past on the streets surrounding the old San Francisco slum. They used the most rudimentary methods to rob: they hid in an alley waiting for a car to drive by, then rushed out in front of it brandishing guns and taking whatever the driver had in his pockets, never more than twenty pesos, which was all they needed to carry on.

In the face of this random violence, neighbors can sometimes react almost spontaneously, as when Brian tried to kill someone. But in other cases, the reaction comes from someone who not only has guns but also has sufficient impunity to take on an enemy regarded as being beyond the pale. In the case of the Sapitos, in the time after Brian was taken away and when the weekend finally came around, the gang members continued crossing boundaries. Not only were they happy to steal from old Don Genaro, a neighbor who lives on the same block as Frente Vital, but they also broke into other houses in the area. Between them, they cleared out a house belonging to relatives of a dealer in the 25 de Mayo slum—a big mistake. After the robbery, the dealer sent them a message saying he would leave them alone if they just brought back the TV and the few other items they had taken. But either they didn't want to or they couldn't. Instead, their response that Saturday was to crack the go-between's skull open with a gun. At dawn on Sunday, they were done for. The dealer gave his nephew the order to take revenge and make it fatal.

To make things worse, the Sapitos were so full of themselves that Sunday that they didn't even stay in their alley or in the few shacks in the slum where they had friends. The guy responsible for gunning down the Sapitos and others had them in his sights: it was just a matter of waiting until they came within range. It was late afternoon when Sapo went and stood on the corner, in full view. The dealer's car coasted by the edge of the slum very slowly, then turned around. Marga, the mai, was in her yard, on the far side of the open ground, when she saw the white car advancing along Quirno Costa Street. It braked sharply on the apartment block sidewalk, and from the car window came bright flashes, like fireworks. "Let's go check it out," she said, and went out. "They've shot Sapito in the head. The car spun around on two wheels, and the shots continued in this direction."

"It's true, the Sapitos had gotten out of control—they'd hit a small child in 25 de Mayo, and they'd tried to mug Don Juan. But I say he should have gotten out of the car to kill him, not done a drive-by shooting from the car like a security guard, like some kind of coward."

At that very moment, Mauro was arriving at the taxi office where he'd been working since getting clean. He had a client to take from the evangelical church to French Street, so he set off in that direction. When he looked out onto the empty lot in front of the apartment blocks, he saw a large group of people and heard desperate cries. On one corner, Sapo lay prone on the grass. Before long, a crowd had surrounded the injured kid. His brother and a friend were calling out to Mauro to stop the car and help them.

"Get him in! C'mon, get him in!" Mauro said, trying to snap them out of their paralysis, when all they could do was to shout at him for help.

Between the Sapito and the girl they lifted the fallen figure, managing to get him into the back seat of the cab. Mauro will never forget the image: the boy's face covered in blood, a sticky liquid seeping from his head where the dealer's hitman had fired the avenging bullet. "I put my foot down, and we sped off. His brother and the woman couldn't stop shouting." It took almost no time, but for Mauro, the scene extends like a nightmare remembered in snatches when you wake up in the middle of the night. He stepped on the gas, certain that saving the boy dying in the back of his car was an impossible mission. Pulling away, he glimpsed the reflection of a window and thought he saw the face of the dying boy begging for salvation in the midst of the living who were crowded around the car. It was Sapito, Sapo's brother, so similar looking that for a moment Mauro confused the two. "But I turned around and saw him with his head blown apart, and then I just accelerated without another thought in my mind." By the time they arrived at the hospital in San Fernando, Sapo was already dead.

"What do you think about his death?" I asked the mai when she told me about that Sunday.

"The only thing I know is that I don't like whoever had him killed. I tell you, if people steal, I give them shelter. But if they sell drugs, I don't want to know them."

"What's the difference?"

"That's easy. If the dealer didn't sell drugs, the kids wouldn't get high and go out stealing. Because the kid who has a clean head uses his mind for other thing, he finds something to do rather than stealing. But the dealer poisons them, and the kids go crazy, stealing and hurting others. You won't hear any mother of a thief say they like dealers. My son was a very good boy, but when he started taking drugs, he was done for."

9

Too many times over the past six years, Nadia left Mauro only to return to live again in the two rooms she shared with him. Too often she felt the urge to go back to her mother's place, leaving the man she fell in love with when she was twenty—the same man she grew to hate, feeling a disgust for him that could be caused only by the deepest of resentments, an unforgivable betrayal, forming in the pit of her stomach. It's strange that, although she detests the pain he has put her through, she still lives with him, in the same place where she has always felt so much ambivalence. She still loves him, still gets jealous when he takes up with other women from the slum—women who flirt and have furtive affairs while their husbands are in prison, despite the risk of provoking a crime of passion.

"I don't see how this can ever be made right," she says, seated in a small chair. Her home, which consists of two rooms and a small store that she opens now and then, is on the paved block of the 25 de Mayo slum, on the path down which Víctor Vital ran on the day of his death, trying in vain to escape the police. She's still convinced that Frente could have saved himself if only he had asked her for shelter that morning. Nadia's face shows the passage of time, the hard knocks of a life shared with Mauro—from the virus she says he gave her knowingly, to the death of one of her nine brothers, two other brothers getting locked away, and the disintegration and collapse of the family they belonged to when kinder winds blew and her parents still dreamed of rising to the middle class.

The disastrous changes began with an economic downfall. The loss of comfort, of social status, and of hope for the future are often the start of an avalanche of losses that can lead, eventually, to death. Nadia was seven years old when it happened. With nine children, her parents lived off the rent of a small apartment and a house in San Fernando. It was a house big enough for all of them: it had a yard, a garden, a utility room, a kitchen, and a dining room. But blind friendship led her father to sign his name as guarantor of a friend's business, and he later invested the money he had saved in a fiberglass pool company. The enterprise turned out to be a mirage that soon evaporated under pressure from creditors and the arrival of hyperinflation. Leaving behind paved streets and sidewalks washed clean every morning, the family found themselves in a shack in the San Francisco of Assisi slum. In spite of the protection of this Catholic saint of the poor, they never managed to emerge from poverty, and Nadia and her brothers became children of the lowest class, with all that that entails. Perhaps it is this coming down in the world that has given Nadia her grim view of what has happened to her and her family over the past few years. Perhaps when Nadia talks about reparations—a word so dear to the discourse of those affected by political repression—this is the highest point of her political demands, the one that brings her the closest to the truth.

"I don't know what you mean when you say *reparation*."

"*Reparation* means a lot of things. First, I'm never going to forgive Mauro for infecting me with the virus. He always said he wasn't infected before he met me. And that's a lie. I try to ignore it, but I can't. And it wasn't a nosy neighbor who told me, it was the doctor: Mauro had had the virus for fourteen years when he ruined me. I think it was at that moment that this hatred was born, the strongest I have ever felt for anyone."

I remember her cleaning the still-open wound of Mauro's peritonitis operation, the passion for her man's abused body. I remind her of that and her swearing softens. "He's like that, a womanizer, and very uptight. He's like that, just like that," she repeats, as a mantra of loving resignation. Their relationship began in the shadow of the prison where they met. She was a slight, pretty girl who would loyally visit her eighteen-year-old brother, imprisoned in Olmos for robbery. Mauro was spending one of his final years in prison there, having earned a number of prison prerogatives and some respect among the rest of the population. Because Nadia's brother Toti was a neighbor from the same hood and the brother of such a desirable brunette, Mauro saved him from the additional punishment of being a pariah inside the jail. The boy's future was uncertain until he met Mauro in Olmos. He was about to be transferred to join the evangelicals on the ground floor, the "little bros," as they're called; he was going to find God, to get shelter. Mauro rescued him and found him a space by his side. When they parted ways, there was a debt of gratitude: Toti was the first messenger Mauro used to reach Nadia during those prison visits. "A certain Maurito asked me to tell you to write to him," he told her.

MAURO HAD SEEN her during visiting hours because he enjoyed the privilege of working in the most sought-after time of the week, the time when loved ones enter the jail. She had a four-month-old daughter by a man she never saw again, and still remembers that she wrote not one letter, but two. In them, she said a number of things and confessed that she was a single mom. But she never got an answer. Mauro swears he never received them. Mauro has always refused to tell her about life inside prison. What she knows, she's heard from others, especially from Toti. He told her that Mauro helped the local kids, that he wasn't just like the other guys. "Whether or not you're a bank robber, if you're a jerk, they're going to beat you up anyhow, you'll be everyone's slave. They were OK, but I don't know how—they had work, school, gym, everything. I think they were OK because every time they got to a wall they tried to escape." Toward the end of my journey in the slum, Mauro confessed to me that whenever he could, he'd try to break out of the penitentiary system by force, using different strategies. In Azul prison he helped lead a revolt that ended up forcing the justice minister to intervene. "We held up school," he told me, describing how they threatened the teachers in one of the classrooms as part of their attempted escape. "When we had only one set of bars to go, we took two hostages, but it wasn't enough. In the end, it took three days before we were transferred."

When Mauro was allowed back on the streets at Christmas in 1996, Nadia had been going out with another guy for some time, and she wasn't living in San Fernando with her family, but in Virreyes. When she visited her parents, Nadia began glancing his way. She kept walking, though she couldn't help but see Mauro's blond mane and hear his compliments, as he praised her beauty in ways that always verged on the offensive. "I knew he was a womanizer and everything, and for a whole year I was having none of it. I dodged him time and again. He'd go looking for me at the clubs, he invited me to his birthday—I was there for two minutes and left. I knew that I liked him, but deep down I could tell he was trouble. I kept him at bay for a year, I did. Then one day I went past with my sister, and he told my niece to send a kiss to her aunt. Something happened then, I don't know what. . . . He awoke something in me—I began to see him as 'Maurito.'"

When she started to accept dates from her suitor, Nadia set clear limits to fend off his advances in a struggle that's usually about the loss of honor among the women of the slum and their men, an honor that cannot be retrieved. For her, the scene that best illustrates her dignity is the time she refused to go to a motel with him.

He took her to the door of the Astor and said, "Let's go in and watch TV." And she said, "No way!"

He didn't like the refusal. He gave her a hard look and wanted to make her feel guilty for upsetting him.

"Go to hell!" Nadia cut him off.

She explains it this way: "If I hadn't done that, if I'd crossed that threshold, then I would have lost all my rights. Because—it's true—it's the woman who decides, because the guy can be a shit, but if the woman opens her legs, the guy is just going to go ahead. Because I told him to go to hell, he started to visit me at home, again and again. If I did go over to see him, it'd be four in the morning and I'd insist he walk me home. I was driving him crazy. . . . Until one day, I stayed, and I stayed, and I stayed. About a month later, I realized I was in over my head."

Nadia was in love for some time, convinced that the best thing was to have a child with Mauro. They agreed to stop taking precautions, but it didn't work. Then she decided to try starting a treatment to become pregnant. That's how she had an HIV test done in February 1999, which came back negative. Seven months later, when she had already left their house once, tired of his lies and mistreatment, a gynecologist at the health center and a neighbor who worked in a community group called To Live Again visited her mother's home to tell her she had to get tested again: they had detected the virus in Mauro. A fungal infection had sprung up in his mouth and nose, and it was ruining his immune system. He went three months without eating. "Where the infection was it was all white and his skin was the color of maté, olive green. He was the living dead, he weighed as little as eighty-three pounds."

Nadia found out and couldn't help doing some calculations. Why hadn't he wanted to have the semen test that the fertility treatment required? When a dog bit him two years earlier, why did he get that doctor's prescription telling him to undertake "preventive medicine" urgently? Nevertheless, just as she still tends to his wounds now, she stayed by him in the hospital, not leaving his side until he was released. And when Mauro came back to his shack, she put up with him for a while longer. "He got himself another mattress and put it on his side of the bed, because he had gotten used to the hospital bed, which was like that, and then I would sleep on the side that was lower down. He didn't want me to touch him: he kept me at a distance and wanted me to look after him all the time. I would go to bed at four a.m., and he would want me to get up at eight a.m. I was already angry for lots of reasons—because for a year and a half before that I'd had to put up with his torture, abuse, blows, womanizing. That's when I rebelled, because I thought: 'This son of a bitch, he screwed up my life, he hits me, he betrayed me. Why am I putting up with him? Die, you son of a bitch!' And I left."

Nadia says that Mauro's family was glad they separated. But nobody knew what to do with the rebel, the strongman of the family, now that he was sick, thin, on the brink of death. Nadia thinks that the loneliness—the private hell that Mauro entered when she left him on his own, with the virus undermining all his defenses, ruining his posture as an indiscriminate and violent macho man—would later bring about a change that allowed her to go back to him. "He suddenly realized that death was for real . . . ," Nadia thinks.

It was only together that they were able to emerge, or to begin to emerge, from the suffering and stigma often attached to carriers of the virus. Nadia has a painful memory of Mauro's sister, fed up with the attacks of the most violent man in the family, spitting out during a row: "Why doesn't he just die, the sick piece of shit!" This is the kind of insult meant to remind you that death is the worst possible fate. "You know you're going to die, you know it, and because you know you're going to die, you'll suffer, and you'll suffer, all the time. It's a permanent death threat that is ridiculous, really, because it's a lie. In my family home it's the same: my sisters, the two who've helped me and stood by me, would bring their kids around over and over: 'Here, spend time with the kids, see them.' And I'd be like, 'I'm not going to die, bitches! Why are you bringing the kids around to visit me when you never did that before?' I'm not going to die. Everyone has this idea that if you have the virus, you'll die quickly and you need to enjoy life now because you don't have much time left." When Nadia saw Mauro again after two months apart, she thought he would drag her across the floor with the fury she knew so well. "He'll kill me, now he'll kill me," she told herself. She was shaking as she approached him. He was like a specter. His skin was still olive colored; his eyes bulged from hollow sockets. He didn't even manage to say anything: he just burst into tears like a child and then repeated, "I'm sorry, I'm sorry," over and over, apologizing for the long list of sufferings he had caused, his betrayal over the virus just one of many evils he had committed in that wretched landscape.

THROUGH MAURO I discovered Nadia, and meeting her brought me closer to the slum's secrets. Its intrigues begin with the stories of her own brothers, three boys out of nine siblings. It may be in Toti's death that the plotline of warring gangs and underhanded police reaches its nadir. According to his siblings, Toti was the sweetest and most thoughtful of the boys in the family, and the one whom Nadia, as the oldest girl, cared for most. Nadia thinks he embarked on a life of crime as a logical consequence of the disintegration of their family after conflict broke out between her impoverished parents. Toti began to work as soon as their need became pressing. He had a good, strong voice and would sing in bars, on street corners—wherever they gave him a few coins or bread—as brazenly as a boy who begs by making a face or show-ing a physical defect. In the fall, he would harvest lemons from a tree near the shantytown and go around selling them door-to-door. "My mom and dad began to fight, and he started to go down a bad path," Nadia tries to explain.

Toti started hanging out with the group on the corner and in the deal-ers' shacks, including Tripa's. He ended up being part of a gang that had a hideout in the Infico, the neighboring block of apartments. After one failed robbery, he was jailed for two weeks in a juvenile institution. With that ar-rest, his ever-more-distant parents realized their son had started using a gun to get money for pills that he bought from a couple central to the history of San Francisco, 25 de Mayo, and La Esperanza: Gladis and Javo. "She brought the pills into the hood, and he sawed off the shotguns for the kids," Sabina had once told me.

Gladis's name, one common in the slums, was always spoken in hushed tones by the people I interviewed. The mai pointed her out, too. Nadia told me about her on the fourth night I visited her place to listen to her stories. "She and her husband sell pills. They've done that all their lives, because whatever happens, they'll never get busted. Gladis brought crack to the slum like twenty years ago. She always was a piece of shit. For a while, they separated; she kicked her husband out and went to live with her security guard brothers, guys who had killed kids in the slum. It was a short break, only a few months, and then she went back to live with her husband. Now the chief of police drives up to her place in his own car. She doesn't just sell pills, but also coke and weed, everything." The couple is central to how things work in the slum, and to my understanding of how the invisible arm of the police works in the area; at first glance, it might seem like the violence is random, but it's actually the consequence of a complex process, at the heart of which is a complicity that forces businesses to go underground if they want to make any kind of profit.

Toti experienced this as a personal penance. He was barely eighteen when he was jailed for the first time as an adult. He had used the motorcycle his father had given Nadia for her quinceañera. The guy riding with him was supposed to steal a tape player, but the police showed up. Toti managed to escape and run to his mother's place to get the bike's papers. When he got back, his partner had turned him in. "It was him, it was him!" the thief said. Nadia says accusingly, "The other kid's mother is a bitch who's been with a few of the security guards, that's why they blamed Toti and the other kid walked away." For that, Toti served a long stretch at Olmos, protected by the guy who would become his brother-in-law, Maurito.

When Toti got out, he was caught only a few weeks later trying to rob a country villa with another gang. This time he was sent to the Escobar police station, where he shared a cell with a few of Luis Valor's men. On August 24, 1995, one of them gave him the chance, almost an order, to escape. "Are you coming, kid?" they asked him; it was an escape set up in exchange for paying several thousand pesos to one of the police chiefs. Twelve men got away, most of them to Brazil. Nadia says that they encouraged Toti to cross the border with them, but the idiot was in love with a girl, so he took shelter with some friends, stayed with the girl, and eventually rented a place. He stayed, missed the boat, and ended up a refugee in the most dangerous territory of all: his own hood.

TOTI DIDN'T GET very far. Over the following months, he stumbled along the same path. He got closer and closer to an inevitable death sentence—the one meted out by those who are so representative of the police mafia it's like they embody it. Toti never managed to become a part of the networks put together by women from the slum like Gladis, or men with multiple illegal ties like Javo, or like Frente Vital's enemy, Tripa. What's more, the madness, hallucinations, and warping effects of the pills were making Toti crazy. Nadia thinks he was already a little off after leaving prison. She still recalls vividly the images of horror her brother recounted to her after he left Olmos. "The police beatings had driven him mad. He told me that in prison, they slit the throat of one dude for some milk and another for a slice of salami. He said he was never going back, that he'd rather die outside."

Soon Toti's madness also became apparent to his mother. It was a few weeks before the end of the year when he confessed to her, petrified, that he had spoken with his dead grandmother and with Miguelito, the mai's dead son.

"They told me not to come to the hood on New Year's because they're going to kill me," he said.

This was five nights before he died.

The warnings from the ghosts haunting Toti were repeated in person by Javo to his mother, two days before the end of the year.

"You'll see what's going to happen to your son," he warned her on a shanty corner.

ON JANUARY 1, Toti was sick of himself and of everyone else. He crossed the alleys of the 25 de Mayo slum clinging to corrugated metal walls and arrived at Gladis and Javo's house with a full clip. He emptied it, shooting at the windows and the door with such poor aim that almost all the bullets bounced back. Yes, the ghosts had warned him. Yes, he believed them. Yes, everyone knew he'd better not set foot in the slum during that holiday season. But that day, Toti was convinced that shooting first was the best, the only thing he could do. Nadia tries to imagine the messages he might have received from the other world. She can't bear to think that an Umbanda spell might have pushed him to certain suicide. What Nadia does know is that the next day, her brother died in an ambush.

She was with her mother downtown, in a toy store buying presents for Three Kings Day.[1] They saw the ambulance that would collect his body go by. That day, they believed the version of events that the police circulated:

---

1 In Argentina, the time when children get most of their Christmas presents is January 6, Twelfth Night. — Trans.

Toti had tried to hold up a sports store, had injured a girl, and had been caught with two other guys. Toti lay dying for nine days in intensive care in San Fernando hospital. After the funeral, a cop came to Nadia's place with an anonymous letter. It refuted the other officers' version and advised her to speak to the witnesses who knew that Toti had been executed. Nadia was able to speak with the guy who was tending the store where her brother went that afternoon. "They were in a cab, driven by the woman who always took them to holdups. When they went past the place and my brother saw the cops, she stopped and jumped out of the car shouting that she was a hostage. The man in the store knew it was a setup to kill Toti and said to him, "Get out of here or they'll kill us both." Toti burst into tears.

Just as it is hard to understand why Toti went and shot up the dealers' place, it isn't easy to comprehend why he ran off from the store and hid behind the bushes next door. The owner of the house spotted him and called the police. "They went in and killed him: they shot him twice in the chest and once in the head, and kicked him all over his body." The police didn't touch the two guys who were with him, though they did arrest two cartoneros who were passing by. "It was all a setup. Betrayal all around. The deal, brokered by Gladis, was for seven thousand pesos. They gave evidence to my mom, but she was too afraid to ever do anything. They told her that they would torch her house, that they would kill us kids, that my dad was going to lose his job because they had contacts at City Hall."

PRISON MACHISMO, CRIMINAL tradition, police files, all the experts, and even the crime reporters perpetuate the myth that the betrayals suffered by thieves are nearly always connected to a woman: "She cheated with someone who is now behind bars, so he arranged to kill the guy." But in reality, betrayal is almost always related to the police. "They arranged to have Toti killed. Marga told us that Gladis had arranged for him to be arrested before. We found out because a security guard gave me a piece of paper and told me to take it to a judge and to Mauro Viale's TV show.[2] The guy said that they had set him up, that we should check out this one court case. He said that the guys who killed my brother had been waiting for him that night, that it was all set up to get him."

---

2 Mauro Viale is a TV news anchor. — Trans.

Nadia tells me the version she's most convinced by. The slum mai told it to her, just like it was the mai who told her the rumors about the trap set for Toti. Convinced that the mai was herself involved in it, Nadia grew tired of listening to her and shouted:

"Stop lying to me or I'll kick your ass!"

From the darkness of her yard, the mai answered:

"What's your problem, you whore?"

"What's your problem, you whore, you old goat!" Nadia retorted, to someone she had always respected.

The mai cursed her:

"You're going to crawl on the ground like a snake, you and that sick faggot of yours, you poor excuse for a thief!"

THREE YEARS LATER, a month after Frente Vital's death, Ignacio, the second of Nadia's three brothers, killed a policeman on the corner of Las Tropas Street. He had just turned sixteen. He's still in prison for that crime.

Nacho was a small kid, the size of a seventh grader. He hung out on the same corner that his brother Toti had and spent his time, with little skill and fewer scruples, stealing whatever was easiest and closest. On the afternoon of March 24, the anniversary of the last military coup in 1976, he and a fifteen-year-old friend had only one thing in mind: getting money to buy drugs from a dealer in 25 de Mayo. They walked less than half a block to point a gun at the owner of a new store. When the man saw them coming, at first he didn't even believe they were thieves. He spoke to them calmly, as if they were his own kids, went up to them, and kicked them out. The kids ran down the middle of the street, and the storekeeper came after them in a car. As if it had been waiting, a cop car patrolling the hood intercepted them as they ran, and they were arrested. One of the two police officers went off with the storekeeper in his car. The other officer, a thirty-year-old corporal, got behind the wheel of the patrol car with the two kids in the back.

He never even managed to start the car. Two shots were heard coming from inside it. One of the kids had fired a revolver into the back of the corporal's head. Where had the gun come from? The police version states that a girl, also a minor, slipped a gun in through the car window when no one was looking. But Nadia swears that's not what happened. "They took it out of a black and blue bag that was in the car, one of the tricks the cops use to fool kids they're going to kill. My brother says that the cop was a sweetheart, saying, 'We're not going to cuff these two little babies.' Those kids are fucking idiots, I want to kill them myself. They never listened to my husband, and he spoke to them both. He can be tough. He told them to stop taking pills, that they'd be lost. But no, they were blind."

"Was your brother out of control?"

"My brother was a jerk who smoked weed on the corner. I tried to set him straight, but it's the dealers who keep the kids hooked. Tripa was one of the worst. If he saw the kids high, he'd start his spiel. 'Go on, jerk, you're scared! Don't you want a Rolex? You've got what it takes—you're a thief, not just any idiot,' and so on. You can't do anything against them, unless you blow them away."

"Who are the guys like Tripa?"

"They're like the cops' stooges. They're the ones between the cops and the thieves. They know about stuff, they know people, they can do everything the cops can do, but better. A kid who crosses Tripa is history. I'm pretty sure it was him who got Frente killed. They'd had a shoot-out a month earlier in the empty field, and then they shot Frente down like a dog. But it doesn't matter, at some point everyone gets a knife in the back, because this is a world that thrives on betrayal, where traitors have it coming to them."

THREE YEARS AFTER the shoot-out between Víctor and Tripa, Manuel and I were walking along a narrow street in La Boca. For the first time, he admitted to me his role in the slum's rivalries: some days earlier, he and another guy had blown apart the Chanos' shack and taken away a rock of coke as loot. We were walking along, and the tattooed skin of his arm brushed against mine as we stepped on the railroad tracks that border the tenements. That's where he finally told me the whole story.

The last battle of this part of the war began early one day in September 2002, Manuel told me. Tripa and another two guys stopped a car going by 25 de Mayo. They wanted money from the driver. While the man was giving them his wallet, they were feeling up the girl who was with him. Two hours later, they tried to hold up the slum's taxi office. The owner escaped to the empty lot, jumping into the air to avoid the bullets they fired at his feet as they roared with laughter. And then half a dozen armed guys came out from the other end of the field to defend him. One of them shot Tripa in the leg. The dealer ran, limping, to shelter, ending up in a shack in the San Francisco slum just yards from where Frente Vital died.

By nightfall, the decision was made. They would hunt Tripa down, no matter what. They put together an arsenal. They all knew each other, over forty guys. Silent as shadows, they took up positions around the slum, cutting off his escape. A dozen of them walked up the alley, half a yard between each of them, spread open like a fan. They walked stealthily, not wanting their footsteps to set the dogs barking. Their plan was to get to the door of the shack, kick it down, and start shooting. They were five yards away, lined up like a firing squad, when suddenly the door creaked. Tripa had needed to go to the bathroom two shacks down, but the pain in his leg was too bad. Thinking he was alone, he dropped his pants to his knees and leaned against the wall, crouching down right there. And right there, in that undignified pose, in the darkness, revenge caught up with him. Four shots rang out, one after the other. He hardly made a sound. His chest bloodied, he let go of his pants and rocked forward, trying to grab hold of the man who had shot him. But then another seven shots knocked him over on his back. While he was lying on the ground, a seventeen-year-old kid put a snubnose .22 to his head and finished him off.

Nadia, who is a huge fan of the reality show *Big Brother*, remembers clearly that that night she had chosen to watch the show *Videomatch* instead. The guest singer was Sebastian with his group, and among the musicians was a kid from the slum. Nadia was watching her neighbor on TV, having fun, when the shots rang out from the other side of the empty lot in the San Francisco slum. First four. Then seven. Then the final one. She felt a wave of nausea rise in her throat, as if she were about to vomit. The TV screen grew blurry. She couldn't understand where the tears were coming from; she knew that lots of people wanted to kill Tripa, that vengeance was just around the corner, that the decision to carry out the killing had been made.

While the gunmen fell back from the corpse, Nadia dried her tears, angry at herself for her compassion. Tripa didn't deserve anyone to feel sorry about his death, she thought, just as the boy who played cumbia with Sebastian gave a shout-out to all those in San Fernando who were watching:

"A big hello to 25 de Mayo!" he shouted.

Soon after that, the police sirens could be heard, wailing like desperate widows as they came to recover the dead body. The number of police cars multiplied. There were so many, people said it looked like it was a police inspector who had been killed. Once more, a fight broke out between the cops and the residents of the slum. Yet another battle. The next day, they had barbecues and played cumbia to celebrate. But the war wasn't over.

On Thursday, February 20, the phone rang, bringing bad news again. It was Sabina. She told me Daniel had died. After six months in a coma in the hospital, Daniel had said good-bye to Matilde and his brothers in silence. The next day, we all gathered for the farewell ceremony at Estela's place, at the end of the usual alley. It was a hot morning. The yard was full of chairs where women who had been up all night were talking in hushed tones. Estela and Matilde were calm, with tear-stained faces. They looked as if they were tired of crying. We hugged Manuel and Simon, who also seemed calm. They had emptied the room of furniture and taken down all of Simon's paintings. The open coffin stood where the table usually was. Women were weeping in a line to one side. On the other side stood the men. The younger ones, Manuel and Simon, came near the box and stared over other people's shoulders at their dead brother, killed by that blow on the white train.

At around midday, the people from the funeral parlor arrived, a bit late because they had been so busy that weekend. The Miranda family closed the coffin and slowly carried Daniel outside. They set off down the alley. The women came out to their doorways to cross themselves. There was barely room for the procession in the narrow alleyway. We set out for San Fernando cemetery in a number of cars and a truck full of people. That Saturday, the paths in the burial ground looked like a highway of death, so many funerals were taking place at the same time. While some arrived with faces contorted in pain, others left holding on to each other, supported with difficulty by relatives and friends. We walked down one of the paths on the left-hand side of the cemetery and went straight to the grave dug for Daniel. Only a few of the members of this procession were crying. It was as if there had been an unspoken order from Matilde, who was as feisty as ever that day. Something like: We've been in mourning for a long time already. Let's not overdo it. Let him rest in peace. Let's go back to daily life, which we shouldn't fear even if death is a frequent visitor.

So we spread out around the grave. We threw in some flowers before the damp earth was shoveled onto the coffin. Just as they finished covering it, another funeral procession came along the same path; in this one, the relatives, especially the women, were disconsolate in their grief. Given the age of the mourners, it looked like it had been a sudden death of someone very young. As the stranger's coffin began to descend to its final resting place, Daniel's mourners began to disperse. The majority had already seen several men in uniform among the neighboring group. It was obvious that the person who had died had been a policeman. I was warned about this by Chaías. Distanced as he was from the Mirandas and his old friends, he turned up toward the end of the ceremony and had seen the cops come in. His eyes were spinning. He also told me it was his birthday.

At the edge of Daniel's grave, the only one who remained after everyone else had left was his father, Pájaro. He had been to see him in hospital but had disappeared months before, one afternoon when he left the intensive care unit saying he would be back with the urgent medication his son needed. The others went back to the cars and the truck. I walked with Sabina, Frente's siblings, and Manuel to the grave of the thief who had brought me to the shantytown such a long time ago. We stood in front of his black and white photo, next to the kids' untouched offerings, by the bottles of Pronto Shake that decorated the tomb. Each of them kissed the photo. I did too. They all crossed themselves. So did I. And then we were all quiet for a good long while. We wept until Sabina told us it was time to go. We returned to La Esperanza slum and had something to eat together. Then, as night fell, I walked to the train station.